Preaching
the New Testament

Preaching the New Testament

A. M. HUNTER

WILLIAM B. EERDMANS PUBLISHING COMPANY
GRAND RAPIDS, MICHIGAN

Copyright © 1963, 1981 A. M. Hunter

First published 1981 by SCM Press Ltd., London
This American edition published 1982 by
Wm. B. Eerdmans Publishing Co., 255 Jefferson Ave., S.E.
Grand Rapids, MI 49503

Library of Congress Cataloging in Publication Data

Hunter, Archibald Macbride.
Preaching the New Testament.

1. Bible. N.T. — Sermons.   2.   Church of Scotland —
Sermons.   3.   Sermons, Scottish.   I.   Title.
BS2361.3.H86   1982   252′.0523   81-19482
ISBN 0-8028-1919-2   AACR2

Contents

Gratis

63833

Preface

When, in 1963, I sent him a MS containing seven New Testament studies plus four lectures on the theology of P. T. Forsyth, the Editor of the SCM Press suggested that I might also include in it, for good measure, a dozen sermons. The resultant book, *Teaching and Preaching the New Testament,* is now out of print.

Then, a few months ago, my friend the Rev. Malcolm Hare, minister of St Kentigern's Church, Kilmarnock, visiting me in the 'land o' Burns', strongly urged me to publish a book of sermons on New Testament themes. At first I demurred; but, on further reflection, yielded to his kind importunity, and was delighted when the SCM Press accepted my MS for publication.

Four of the dozen sermons in the 1963 volume reappear in this one, slightly amended. The remaining thirty are new. They include sermons preached at the General Assembly of the Church of Scotland and to the Royal Family at Crathie Church, besides others preached in Oxford, Perth, Aberdeen and in the United States.

The themes are many and various – from 'Christian Faith and the Riddle of the World' to 'The Holy City' – besides studies of Christ's greatest parables, and his teaching on prayer, plus addresses suitable for Good Friday, Easter Day, and Whitsunday, as well as sermons on the church and sacraments, the Christian ethic and eternal life.

The only merit I claim for them is that they are based on long and careful New Testament exegesis, and that their main aim is to make 'the old, old story' Good News for sin-sick and bewildered modern man. For, as I understand the matter, Christian preaching is essentially 'the Gospel prolonging and declaring itself'

(P. T. Forsyth). It is the dynamic medium through which today, by the Holy Spirit's working, God contemporizes his saving self-disclosure in Christ his Son, and offers us the opportunity of responding to it by faith, which is a taking of God at his redeeming Word in Christ, incarnate, crucified, risen, and now regnant in the highest place that heaven affords.

It is my conviction that one prime cause for the church's decline today is the lack of truly evangelical preaching based firmly on the Good News of the apostles. Too often, I fear, our preachers tend to substitute a secularizing social ethic, or what our forefathers would have called 'cauld blasts of morality', for the Gospel which St Paul defined as 'God's way of righting wrong'. The cure for this is to put back Christ and the Gospel (which is about divine salvation for sinners) into the centre of our preaching.

If these thirty-four sermons, for all their imperfections, can help not only our ministers but also lay-preachers and what we now call 'non-stipendiary priests', to return to the great themes of the New Testament and proclaim them to their congregations in words and idioms which will come home to their hearers, I shall be well satisfied.

Once more I offer my warm thanks to my old friend and now near neighbour, the Rev. David G. Gray, for his careful scrutinizing of both typescript and proofs.

3 *Carwinshoch View*,   A. M. Hunter
Ayr

I

Christian Faith and the Riddle of the World

(John 1.1–18)

What does it mean to see God and the world through Christian eyes?

You can divide all mankind up into two classes – one-world people and two-world people. The first believe only in this visible world they can touch and see. The others – the two-world people – believe also in an invisible world, a world lying beyond the curtain of their senses, the world of God.

Christians are two-world people. They believe not only that God exists but that he has revealed himself to men, above all, in Jesus Christ his Son. Their response to this divine revelation they call 'faith', and by it they believe they are enabled to find answers to those great ultimate questions which men have been asking from time immemorial.

I

First: *How did this visible world come into existence?* To this question, they say, there is only one right answer – the first four words of Genesis, 'In the beginning, God.' For what is the alternative? Why, that this world just happened by sheer chance. Very well, but the world, as we know it, is governed by natural laws, like the law of gravity – 'What goes up must come down.' But, if the laws of nature exist by sheer chance, may not tomorrow alter them completely? 'Nonsense!' the plain man will reply. Exactly. To deny the creation of the world by a Supreme Being is to land in the non-sense of atheism. Let us not, however, confuse the *fact* of creation with the process. If we want to know *how* the

1

world was made, we may ask the scientists for their latest views. Did not Albert Einstein, the greatest of them all, say of his famous 'relativity theory', 'I want to know how God created this world – I want to know his thoughts – the rest are details'?

Religion deals with the fact. Even if we cannot understand it, it is in this respect like many other facts in it – to take two obvious and everyday examples, the marvellous instinct of the homing pigeon, or of the mature salmon coming back from somewhere near the North Pole to spawn in the river where it was born.

II

Question No 2: *Why did God create the world?*
For an answer I bid you consider that by the testimony of both the Bible (Gen. 1) and of evolution, man is the highest form of 'life on earth', the crown of God's creation. It would appear, then, that God made the world primarily (though not exclusively) for man's sake.

Again, don't get confused with the *how*. The process whereby the human race has reached its present state is a matter for the scientists. Stick to the fact. Religion deals with the fact and its meaning, namely, that man was evidently God's primary object in view at the creation of the world.

If you agree thus far, let us also agree that God did not just create the world and then proceed to forget all about it, like some absent-minded old professor. Did not the man who knew God better than any other born of woman say, 'My Father has never yet ceased his work, and I am working too' (John 5.17)?

III

So to Question No 3: *If God created the world primarily for man's sake, what is God's concern for it now?*
Before we answer, we must face two further facts. The first is *the fact of evil*. Today this needs no proving. All we need do is to look in at 'News at Ten'. Only a starry-eyed optimist, turning a blind eye on all the evil around him, would call this world an earthly paradise. Nor does it need much wit to perceive that the evil is not just in our circumstances but in ourselves.

Now, evil, in a personal and individual sense, is *sin*, sin which

2

is not so much what we do as what we *are*. And sin, however much we try to explain it away (e.g. as 'humanity's growing pains'), remains a stubborn, ungainsayable fact. Once again, don't get side-tracked with speculations about its origin. The plain truth is that, however many have been men's theories about it, it abides a mystery: we only know that it is there. Stick to the fact that what our forefathers called 'original sin' is something very real, and that we are all involved in it, like runners in the strawberry bed. It was not a theologian but a politician, the late Richard Crossman, who said: 'To judge by the present state of the world, there is a good deal more evidence for the Christian doctrine of "Original Sin" that there is for Rousseau's doctrine of the noble savage or Karl Marx's of the classless society.'

The second fact to be faced, the fact of *man's need*, arises from his sinfulness. Sin lodges at the centre of his being, warps his will, and disables his endeavours after good. Of course we don't like to admit this. We would like to think that we can cure ourselves of this malaise – without divine assistance. We cherish the hope that maybe science, psychology, or higher education will rid us of it, this thing the Bible calls 'sin'. But it is a forlorn hope. There is no human remedy for the curse of sin.

IV

So to our last question: *Can God help us?*

Here argument really comes to an end. Our reason can take us so far – to the edge of the gap, so to speak. Now all argument is useless unless we are ready to take a leap – the leap of Christian faith. A blind leap? On the contrary, one whose rightness has been confirmed by countless Christians down the centuries. For, having taken the leap, they have found that it brought them what they needed for their souls' sore hurt.

Here Paul is the example *par excellence*. In his letter to the Romans he has told us how, before his conversion, he strove earnestly, by keeping all the laws of Moses, to 'get right with God', and how always he failed miserably to find the peace of mind for which he longed. The good he willed he could not do, and the evil which he hated that he did. Why? Because (he says), sin lodging at the very centre of his being, frustrated all his best

3

endeavours. 'O wretched man that I am,' he cried despairingly 'who shall deliver me from this body doomed to death?'

Then Paul made the leap. 'Who shall deliver me?' he had said, and the answer came when he came face to face with the risen Christ on the Damascus Road: 'God will – through Christ!' And in place of dejection and despair came that sense of pardon, peace and power that was to send Paul across half the known world to tell men of God's Good News in Christ his Son.

'God will – through Christ!' – this is what we must believe if we want to know how God can meet man's deepest need. The Gospel proclaims that Christ, the Son of God, died, by his Father's appointment, for the sins of men, and that through Christ, who is now alive for ever, man can be brought back into a family relationship with God, and that this relationship, begun here on earth, is hereafter to be continued and perfected in a Father's house on high.

But, to prove the truth of this, we must first make that leap called 'faith'.

Let us sum up our enquiry with a true story. At the first meeting called to found the YMCA, somebody proposed that it should be named 'The Young Men's Religious Association'. Whereupon one of its founders, George Williams, took his pen, stroked out the word 'religious' and wrote instead 'Christian'. Williams knew what he was doing. Mere vague, nebulous religiosity will take you nowhere: without that leap of commitment to Christ, God will remain for you at best the Honorary President of the universe, a being cold and remote as the stars.

With that commitment, God becomes for you the Father of Christ and, through him, your Father also. But make the leap you must.

What then is Christian faith? It is 'the grand venture' in which we commit ourselves and our future to the conviction that Jesus Christ is not an illusion but the reality of God, and that in him the All Highest has spoken his Word for our salvation.

2

Why be a Christian?

(I Peter 3.15)

If a man asks you why you are a Christian, wrote St Peter, always be ready to give him an intelligent answer, but (he added) do so modestly and reverently.

That was nineteen hundred years ago, when Christianity was facing persecution at the hands of the Roman Empire, personified in the wicked Emperor Nero. Today, when it is once more on trial, and Christian beliefs and morals are once again under fire, is not the same readiness being demanded for us?

Suppose one day a communist or a humanist were to ask you, 'Why are you a Christian?' How would you answer him?

If I were asked that question, my questioner would not, I think, be much impressed if I proceeded to talk to him about the Incarnation, the Atonement, or the Triunity of God, basic though these doctrines are to our faith. He would want much simpler, less theological, reasons for taking the Christian view. What then? If that question were put to me, there are three things I should want to say in my reply; and maybe, if we discuss them now, they will help others to find answers of their own.

I

First, then, I am a Christian because Christianity makes sense for me of the riddle of existence.

Why are we here at all? What is the meaning of this strange bitter-sweet thing we call life? And to what mysterious shore are we steering our fragile little ships?

These are the great ultimate questions with which every man or woman who takes life seriously must make his, or her, reckoning. Old questions, to be sure, but ever new ones, for they confront

5

us with fresh poignancy and power every time there is crisis or calamity in our land or in these lives of ours. And for these questions, in my view, there is but one satisfying answer, that given by the poet William Wordsworth:

> One adequate support
> For the calamities of mortal life,
> Exists, one only, an assured belief
> That the procession of our fate, howe'er
> Sad or disturbed, is ordered by a Being
> Of infinite benevolence and power
> Whose everlasting purposes embrace
> All accidents, converting them to good.

Is not this, in essence, the Good News of the Gospel? At the heart of ultimate reality dwells an almighty Father who has 'made us for himself', and who, in Christ his Son, is seeking to reconcile a sinful world to himself. What he desires and designs is a great human family living for ever in fellowship with himself, and trained for their eternal destiny by the disciplines of earth.

'It is for discipline that you have to endure,' says the writer to the Hebrews; 'God is treating you as sons· for what son is there whom his father does not discipline?' (Heb. 12.7). Here on earth, by joy and by sorrow, by happiness and by suffering, we are being disciplined and trained, in order that we may be fit persons to receive all those blessed things which our heavenly Father has in store for those who love him.

This, or something very like it, is the Christian solution to the riddle of our existence. This life of ours is a kind of education which God our Father puts us through.

Mysteries of course remain, and always will, on this side of eternity. Here on earth, as St Paul said, 'we know only in part'. But for those who are humble enough to accept the good news of the Gospel, they become mysteries not of darkness but of *light*. And, in God's great hereafter, shall we not 'know', even as also we are now 'known'?

II

For a second reason, I am a Christian because Jesus Christ is for me 'the Lord of all good life'.

Ever since man became conscious of the difference between right and wrong, he has been pondering the question, 'How ought I to live?' 'What is the good life?' It is because Christ's design for living – as you find it, for example, in his Sermon on the Mount – is incomparably the best that I call him 'the Lord of all good life'.

Better than any other he tells us how to live, how to treat our neighbours, our friends, our enemies. He makes 'love' (*agapē*) the master-key of morals; and by 'love' he means a selfless 'caring' for others, a total devotion to the other man in his need. He sums up the whole duty of man to his fellow man in his 'Golden Rule': 'Always treat others as you would like them to treat you.' He teaches that true greatness lies in readiness to serve, and himself, as the Servant of God, goes to the cross to save men from their sin.

And all through his ministry on earth as recorded in the gospels I find goodness, humility, compassion, gentleness and truth such as I find in no other born of woman. In short, when I consider his life and study his teaching, I cannot doubt that that is how God would have us live.

But Christ gives me more than pattern; he gives me also power. He not only shows me what the good life is, but he helps me with the living of it. For, since his resurrection, Christ is now a living Lord who comes, unseen but not unknown, through the Holy Spirit, as day by day, committing myself afresh to him, I find by experience that I am enabled to lead a better life; and though I may never be able to cry with St Paul, 'I can do all things in (union with) him who strengthens me', I know very well that without his help I should be a worse man than I am.

Here, then, is a divine pattern for living and a divine master to help with the living of it, that need not fear comparison with any other.

III

Finally, I am a Christian because Christianity holds out the blessed hope of everlasting life.

In other words, in Christ and the Gospel I find the best grounds for believing that death is not an end but a beginning, not a terminus but a milestone on an endless road.

To be sure, I may find support for my belief in an afterlife elsewhere: in the ineradicable human instinct, found in every age and race, that the dead live on; in the arguments of the philosophers from Plato to Kant; perhaps even in some of the better evidence provided by the spiritualists. But, when I am asked to give a reason for 'the hope that is in me', it is upon two strong pillars in the Christian temple of truth that I rest my confidence.

The first is *the character of God* as he has revealed himself in Christ. If God is such a Father as Christ declared him to be, loving us with an invincible love and prepared to give up his only Son for our saving, he cannot allow 'the last enemy' to break for ever the strong bands that bind us to himself.

Are we to believe that the purposes of the good and wise Father above will be defeated by a germ, by a fall of coal, or perhaps by a surgeon's mistake? No, no, when God loves once, he loves for ever, loves us with a love that will not let us go even at the last frontier of human existence; and death, for the Christian, is not a passing into nothingness – not a candle blown out never to be relighted, but, as it was for Christ himself, a going to be with the Father in his house with many rooms.

The second strong pillar is *the resurrection of Christ himself* With a full knowledge of the evidence for that supreme event, I cannot doubt that Christ conquered death and showed himself alive to many witnesses. I am persuaded that he is living now. I remember his promise to his followers, 'Because I live, you will live also.' And I take to myself that promise and wait for the time when it will come true.

On these two pillars – the strong love of God and the fact of a living Christ – I build my immortal hope.

We started from the need to give the enquirer reasons for the faith and hope that are in us. I have not exhausted the answers, but have I given you a basis for answers of your own? Can you say with me, 'I am a Christian because Christianity makes sense for me of the mystery of life, because it gives me a Lord and Master whom any man might be proud to serve, and because it holds out the "lively hope" that death, so far from being the ending of the road, is but the gateway to a Father's house on high'?

8

That creed I fain would keep,
That hope I'll not forgo,
Eternal be my sleep –
Unless to waken so.

3

What think ye of Christ?

(Matt. 22.42)

One day in London some distinguished writers of the time fell
to discussing 'persons they would like to have met'. When most of
the great names had been mentioned, up rose Charles Lamb and
said, in his stuttering way, 'There is only one person I can ever
think of after this. If Shakespeare were to come into this room,
we should all rise up to meet him. But, if that person were to come
into it, we should all fall down and try to kiss the hem of his
garment.'

Lamb felt about Christ, as we are told his first followers felt
about him, that there was something uncanny – something not
of this world – in his person. In his way, he was posing the question
of questions, 'What think ye of Christ? Whose Son is he?'

I

It is this question which is before us now. Let us begin our answer
by saying that, if ever there was 'a sound mind in a sound body',
it was Christ's. Sanity and sagacity mark all his moral teaching.
Though never blind to the evil lurking in the human heart, he
yet summoned his followers to the good, the God-like life, in sayings whose sapience and sublimity men have ever since freely
acknowledged. Said the great German Goethe: 'I bow before
Christ as the divinest manifestation of the highest principle of
morality.' Well known is the deep debt that Gandhi, India's
greatest son, owed to Christ's Sermon on the Mount. Even today
those humanists who preach 'morals without religion' are not
foolish enough to decry the morality which Christ taught.

Here then is the problem: how are we to reconcile the sanity
and sublimity of Christ's moral teaching with the quite stupendous

10

claims which he made for himself in the ways of God with men?

Consider only a few of them.

He claims to be the fulfiller of the Law and the Prophets, that is, the whole historic self-revelation of God made to old Israel.

He declares that he has come to set the earth aflame with the heavenly fire.

He comes forward as the divine pardon incarnate, saying to men and women, 'I forgive your sins'.

He claims to be God's only Son and the sole revealer of his unseen Father in heaven.

He asserts that upon men's acceptance or rejection of himself and his teaching depends their eternal destiny.

In the upper room, as he hands the wine-cup to his disciples, saying, 'This cup is the New Covenant sealed by my blood,' he claims that, by his death for sinners, he will inaugurate the new and blessed order of relations between God and man prophesied by Jeremiah centuries before.

When, at his trial, the High Priest asks him, 'Are you the Christ, the son of the Blessed One?', he answers, 'I am', and goes on to predict that, despite the apparent ruin of his cause, he will yet be gloriously vindicated. 'I shall be received by God,' he tells his judge, 'to the highest place that heaven affords.'

What other man in his senses ever made such staggering claims for himself? In vain you will search the other great religions of the world for a parallel. As C. S. Lewis put it, 'If you had gone to Buddha and asked him "Are you the son of Brahma?" he would have said, "My son, you are still in the vale of illusion." If you had gone to Mohammed and asked him, "Are you Allah?", he would have rent his clothes and then cut your head off. If you had asked Confucius, "Are you Heaven?", he would have replied, "Remarks which are not in accordance with nature are in bad taste." '

This, then, is the issue: on the one hand, Christ's sane and noble moral teaching; on the other, those claims of his which, if they are not true, are those of the greatest megalomaniac of all time. The person who makes them is either a madman, or he is divine.

11

II

Here, however, the sceptic may demur: 'Did Christ in fact make these tremendous claims for himself? Are they not mostly the inventions of his followers?'

To this objection the answer is that no documents in all history have ever been subjected to such rigorous criticism as the gospels, and that, after it all, their essential trustworthiness remains unshaken. 'It is of no use,' wrote John Stuart Mill, no conventional Christian, 'to say that Christ as exhibited in the gospels is not historical, and that we do not know how much of what is admirable in them has been added by his followers. Who among his disciples, or their converts, was capable of inventing the sayings ascribed to him, or of imagining the life and character revealed in the gospels?'

III

But, when we have said all this, we are not yet at the end of our enquiry. Still to consider is the sequel which the gospels go on to relate.

What is the true significance of Christ's resurrection? Some have taken it to be just another, though a remarkable, piece of evidence, for the old belief that human personality can survive the shock of death. Not thus do the apostolic writers, Paul, Peter and the rest, regard it. Read their letters, and you will see that they regarded it as something unparalleled in the story of mankind. One man, by God's power, had left one gaping tomb in the wide graveyard of the world; and his triumph over death was like the breaching of a North Sea dyke, an event of seeming slight importance whose consequences were yet cosmic. For if one, and he the man who carried in his own person the whole future of God's people, had exploded the myth of death's invincibility, a new creation had begun, bringing with it 'newness of life' for all who were his, with the hope hereafter of immortal life in that heaven where he now lived and reigned.

IV

'What think ye of Christ?' We have briefly considered the evidence of the New Testament. What is to be our verdict on Mary's

12

son, the man who is at the very centre of the gospel story? Once, in the days of his flesh, he himself had asked his disciples this question, 'But who do you say that I am?' Then Peter, the 'Rock man', speaking for the rest, had replied, 'Thou art the Christ, the Son of the living God!' This is the Christian answer to our opening question, 'What think ye of Christ? Whose son is he?', as it finds expression in the noble affirmations of the *Te Deum*:

Thou art the King of Glory, O Christ: thou art the everlasting Son of the Father . . . when thou hadst overcome the sharpness of death, thou didst open the kingdom of heaven to all believers.

V

One word more: not mine but that of one of the greatest of all Christians, St Augustine: 'You must believe,' he wrote, 'if you would understand.' It is a true saying: to know a person, 'you must first love him, ere to you he will seem worthy of your love.'

Down nearly twenty centuries worship and adoration no less than thinking and theorizing have led Christians to 'the truth as it is in Jesus'. If then what the New Testament and the creeds have to say about Christ is to be accepted, there must be a personal response to the challenge with which God confronts us in his Son.

To the natural man, in the pride of his intellect, this sounds absurd. He supposes that the mystery of Christ's person is to be solved intellectually, without any idea of self-commitment to him. Long experience shows him to be mistaken. Take the natural man's approach, and Christ will remain for you an enigma. Only faith and love know who he really is, and Christian faith is the decision to commit your whole soul and future to the confidence that Christ is not an illusion but the reality of God.

4

What is Christianity?

(Col. 1.4f.)

Suppose one day you were sitting on a Brains Trust when the question-master put the question, 'What is Christianity?', how would you answer?

Is Christianity a creed to be believed? Is it a life to be lived? Or is it a means of getting a passport into heaven?

One man will tell you that what you believe is what really matters. Another will say, 'I don't give a fig for your creeds. The life's the thing.' And another will tell you that the chief thing is to be 'saved', that is, to be sure that you are going to heaven.

Are all these answers quite wrong? Surely not. But surely also none of them is big enough, deep enough, comprehensive enough. But if so, where are we to look for an authoritative answer?

When you are faced with a difficult question in law, or science or economics, you don't go to Tom, Dick, or Harry for an answer. If you are a wise man, you seek out an expert, an expert on the subject. Well, here is a difficult question – so let us consult an expert. And to whom can we better go than to St Paul, well named as 'the fifth evangelist'? St Paul was an expert on Christianity. He taught it; he lived it; and finally he died for it. And I suggest that you won't find a better clue to the answer we are seeking than in those three little words to which Paul keeps coming back again and again in his letters – I mean, faith, love and hope. If we can find out what he meant by these words, we shall be well on the way to an answer.

I

The first thing is 'faith'. Faith is of the essence of Christianity. But what does Christian faith mean?

14

Well, though faith is one of those words that can mean many things – from blind credulity to barren orthodoxy – there is no doubt what St Paul meant by it. It was 'faith in Christ Jesus' (as the text says). It was directed not to a proposition but to a person – a living person. It was utter trust in the living Christ – the Christ who had died, by his Father's appointing, to save men from their sins. And once, in his letter to the Galatians, he defined it. 'The life that I now live in the flesh,' he wrote, 'I live by faith.' What kind of faith? 'Faith in the Son of God who loved me and gave himself for me.'

But how does a man come by such a faith? 'Faith,' Paul answers, 'comes from hearing' – hearing the Gospel. And a man comes to such a faith when he responds with all his heart to the Good News of God's grace to sinners in the cross. When a sinful man – and we are all sinners – hears the story of the cross aright – when, as he gazes upon 'that strange man' hanging there, he sees not simply one more Jew dying a malefactor's death but the very God himself bearing in his Son the sin of the world – when, as he 'surveys the wondrous cross', there breaks upon his soul the revelation 'God loves like that!', what is the man to do? If a man, with the sense of his own sin upon him, once sees the cross like that, there is only one thing for him to do – to surrender himself to that sin-bearing love of God which confronts him in the cross, and to do so unconditionally, unreservedly, and for ever.

Yes, for ever. For Christian faith is not the act of a moment only, but the attitude of a whole life. It is not merely once to affirm, 'I believe in Jesus Christ as my Lord and Saviour', but to go on believing in him day after day, year after year, counting that the highest wisdom God has given you under his visiting moon. This is Christian faith – 'the grand venture' in which we commit our whole soul and future to the conviction that Christ is not an illusion, but the reality of God, his Word to us for time and for eternity.

II

So to the second part of our text: 'the love which you have to all the saints', that is, 'all God's people'. Faith and love belong

15

together. If faith is one side of the medal, love is the other. 'Faith' says St Paul, our expert, 'works through love' – finds expression in love, flowers in love – or it is not faith at all but a sham and a husk – 'Though I have all faith,' says the apostle, so that I could remove mountains, and have not love, I am nothing.'

But what does he mean by 'love'?

The Greek language which he wrote has three main words for 'love'. First, *erōs*. This is the love that craves and, at its lowest, lusts. You will not find it in the New Testament. Next, there is *philia*, 'friendship' – mutual affection between kindred spirits, like David and Jonathan. You will find it but once in the New Testament. The third word is *agapē* – and the New Testament resounds with it. *Agapē* is the love which seeks not to possess but to give, to spend and be spent for the object beloved. If *erōs* is all take, and *philia* is give-and-take, *agapē* is all give. This is Paul's word for 'love'.

Is it then some kind of emotion? No, there is nothing sloppy or sentimental about it. True, there may come situations where *agapē* may be associated with emotion, but *agapē* is something more. This something more can be expressed by no less a word than life. Christian love is the new way of living that came into the world with Christ, so that pagan men exclaimed, 'See how these Christians love one another!' It is a new way of living for God and for our fellow men because God has loved us in Christ. Such love is the way of life for all who call Christ Saviour. It is the energy we are called on to radiate among our fellow-men. 'By this,' said Christ, 'shall all men know that you are my disciples, if you have love one to another.'

III

The last of the little words is 'hope': 'the hope which is laid up for you in heaven'.

The early Christians, we are told, 'spoke to each other softly of a hope' – the hope of the final consummation of God's kingdom and Christ's coming in the glory of his Father. Today, I fear, hope tends to become the Cinderella in our trinity of Christian graces, though this weary, war-torn world needs it more than

16

ever. Certainly it does not hold the place in many Christians' thinking today that it held in the glad springtime of our faith. Again and again in the New Testament that radiant little word rings out with the note of a joy-bell. We read of 'the God of hope', 'the hope of the Gospel', 'Christ Jesus our hope'. St Peter speaks of 'the living hope' which is ours ever since Christ rose from the dead. And the writer to the Hebrews calls hope 'a sure and steadfast anchor of the soul', because the ascended Christ has himself made it fast for us, within the veil, in his Father's heaven.

New Testament hope, be it noted, is never a vague, nebulous optimism that somehow in the end things will turn out all right. Ever it is religious hope – hope which rests not on man but on the living God, the Father of Jesus Christ.

Now turn to the text: 'the hope which is laid up for you in heaven'. Here the word 'hope' really stands for the *object* of hope, that is, the heavenly blessedness which God has prepared for those who love him and do his will.

Now such a hope is, or ought to be, immensely important for our present living, ought to be to our souls what oxygen is to our lungs. Robert Louis Stevenson somewhere recalls a conversation which he had with a Fife labourer who was cleaning a cowshed (or, as we say in Scotland, 'mucking a byre'). They talked of many things, and especially of the aims and ends of life. And, as they conversed, says Stevenson, one casual but memorable remark revealed that labourer for the Christian man he was: 'Him that has aye something ayont,' he said, 'need never be weary.' That man knew by spiritual instinct what the New Testament means by 'hope'.

What is the essence of Christianity? Do I go far wrong if I sum it up as faith in God through Jesus Christ, the living Crucified, plus love – *agapē* – to our fellow men, plus the blessed hope of everlasting life?

The practical questions remain, as they always do. Do we hold that faith – or, rather, does that faith hold us? If it does, then the next question 'Do we walk in love? ought to answer itself. And, if we hold that faith and walk in love, we can leave the rest to the God and Father of Christ. For it is the hope of the Gospel that those who 'live by faith in the Son of God', who are united to him by faith as by fetters of adamant, shall one day see him as he is in glory everlasting.

5

The Waiting Father

(Luke 15.11–32)

Were a vote taken to decide which was the greatest of our Lord's parables, there is little doubt that 'the Prodigal Son', as we call it, would top the poll. Why did he tell this story, to whom did he address it, and what has it to say to us today?

According to St Luke, it was one of his ripostes, or rejoinders, to the Scribes and Pharisees of the day who had criticized Jesus for opening the gates of God's kingdom to outcasts and sinners. But how is it to be interpreted? And is it really the parable of the Prodigal Son?

The only explanation which makes sense of the story is that the father represents God, the elder brother the Scribes and Pharisees, and the younger brother the tax-gatherers and social outcasts whom Jesus had befriended. In the parable therefore, God, by the lips of Jesus, declares his free forgiveness for the penitent sinner, while still at the same time gently rebuking the self-righteous Pharisees.

Our old name for the parable is therefore misleading. Some have proposed to re-name it the story of 'the Two Lost Sons'. There is some force in this: for, if the younger son was lost in 'the far country', the elder was no less lost behind a barricade of self-righteousness. But the title 'the Two Lost Sons' also gets the parable out of focus: for the chief character in it is neither of the sons but the father. Right up to the very last scene in the little drama – his moving interview with the elder brother – the father broods over the whole story. Call it then, as one writer does, 'the parable of the Father's love', or still better, as another does, 'the Waiting Father'. It does not really matter, for the father

19

waits because he loves, and the father indubitably represents God.

II

Jesus' parables are stories from real life. (This is one thing which distinguishes them from 'allegories' which have a way of straying into some 'Never Never Land'.) To this our parable seems no exception. They had prodigal sons in Jesus' day. We still have them – the young men (and women) who say, 'Why can't I get away from parental control for a bit – the old man, or the old woman, is getting on my nerves – and see life and the world for myself before settling down?' In the same way, every generation has its 'far country', and one of its names today is 'Hippie Land'.

Yes, but if this is a story from real life, it is more. Some people have supposed Jesus to be saying in this parable, 'This is how an earthly father would treat his returning prodigal. And will not the Good Father above?' But is this, in fact, how ordinary human fathers always welcome home their returning prodigals? Do they run to meet them, embrace and kiss them, load them with new clothes and expensive presents, and reward them with a barbecue and a ball?

Perhaps you have heard the story of the modern prodigal who, on turning up in the 'far country' of a neighbouring parish, was advised by the local minister to 'go back home and his father would kill the fatted calf for him'. The prodigal did so. Later, meeting the minister again, he was asked hopefully, 'Well, and did your father kill the fatted calf for you?' 'No,' came the rueful reply, 'but he nearly killed the prodigal son.'

Who will deny that it often happens so, even in this 'permissive society' of ours?

Our point is that Jesus' story is larger than life. The father of the prodigal is *not* any ordinary father but a quite extraordinary one. What Jesus is here depicting is the extravagant love of God – his sheer grace – to undeserving men.

III

Yet, if our ears are properly attuned, we may hear more in the parable than this. Many of Jesus' parables contain what our scholars call 'implicit christology', that is, veiled hints of whom he knew himself to be – the promised Messiah or Saviour. This parable is one such. It is not only a story about the grace of God; it is a veiled hint that its teller is acting for God, making the divine goodness and grace real to men. 'What I am doing,' says Jesus, in effect, to his critics, 'represents God's nature and will. In this ministry of mine God's love for penitent sinners is being actualized.' In a word, Jesus is claiming to be God's 'apostle', or 'special messenger', to men. Who then is this, we may well ask, who knows himself to be the sheer goodness and grace of God in Galilean flesh and blood?

IV

Just at this point, as we are bringing Christ into the parable, somebody may protest: 'But there is no cross in the parable. It proclaims the free forgiveness of God for the penitent. Is not this the real heart of Jesus' Gospel, and the doctrine that "Christ died for our sins" just a mystification introduced into a simple Gospel by that arch-corrupter of it, Paul of Tarsus?' (Still today, in their ignorance, do some men malign the great apostle.)

To this we may rightly reply that 'Christ died for our sins' was *not* a doctrine which Paul invented, but, as I Cor. 15.3ff. shows, the first article in the earliest Christian creed, and one accepted by all the apostles.

Yet here it is perhaps more relevant to remember that, as a rule, a parable makes only one point, and that we must not expect to find in it the whole Gospel. In fact, the Gospel parables form a kind of running commentary on a great campaign – the Kingdom of God against the kingdom of evil – which took Jesus eventually to the cross. Jesus did not utter his full purpose – which was God's purpose – in this or indeed in any other parable. He uttered it in the last thing he did, the end which crowned his earthly work, and of which he cried in triumph, 'It is finished!' For there came a time when words – even supreme parables – were of no avail, when only a deed could effect what God had sent him into the world to do. That deed was the cross on which, by his Father's appointing, he gave his life as 'a ransom for many' (Mark 10.45).

Our parable speaks of the grace of God to sinners. The cross *is* that grace of God in final and decisive action, God's great parable acted out in the stuff of human history, a parable whose meaning Paul took perfectly when he said: 'God shows his love towards us, in that while we were yet sinners, Christ died for us' (Rom. 5.8).

V

How then are we to make the parable speak its truth to modern man and convince him that the Gospel has the answer to his need?

First, let the younger son stand for all those today who, fed up with the 'establishment' and impatient of 'law and order', rebel against them and resolve to have their fling. Likewise, let the elder son stand for all the unadventurous, conventional Christians who turn a cold, disliking eye on all their contemporaries with their rebellious instincts.

To those stay-at-home Christians – 'those dull, prissy paragons', as the prodigals might style them – who complain that they have always done what they should but have never had any bright lights in their lives, the Father of the parable is saying, 'Son, you are always with me, and all that is mine is yours.' If then you happen to be in the elder brother's shoes, give God thanks for all your blessings, and be grateful that you have escaped all the heartache and hopelessness of your contemporaries.

And to the modern prodigals the father (who is God) is saying: 'You chose freedom, and I did not stop you. All the time you have been in the far country I have been worrying about you. And here I am still, waiting to welcome you home.'

For the abiding truth of Christ's greatest story is that behind the drift and destiny of human affairs and brooding over them in compassion is a gracious heavenly Father, and that, as the greatest returned prodigal of all, St Augustine, put it, 'Our hearts will never find rest until they find it in him.'

Thus the last secret of the parable is this. There can be a home-coming for us all, because there is a home. The door which leads to the Father's house with its 'many rooms', stands ever open, as there is one who has died and risen to open it, and who still today says, as he said long ago, 'I am the true and living Way to the Father.' The decisive – the existential – question is: 'Do we want

Great!

to come home?' For, as P. T. Forsyth said, truly, summing up the long debate about predestination and free-will: 'We are all predestined in love to life, sooner or later – *if we will*.'

6

The Good Employer

(Matt. 20.1–15)

Christ's tale about the labourers in the vineyard recalls the old
'Feeing Fairs' in our land when farmworkers, seeking employ-
ment, would meet their potential employers. A bargain would be
struck, conditions agreed, and a wage fixed. But, though the setting of Christ's parable is the market-place, which was the em-
ployment exchange of the day, is it really, as some have supposed,
a story about 'the just wage'?

The short answer is: the grumblers in the story are the Pharisees
who complained that Jesus was opening the gates of God's Kingdom to all kinds of dubious characters known as 'publicans and
sinners', and the parable is a proclamation of the great grace of
God.

But to the tale. It was autumn in Palestine and time to gather
in the grape harvest. Since the rainy season was near, speed was of
the essence, with the more hands the better. So, one morning, at
6 a.m., the owner of the estate (whom we will call 'the employer')
set out to engage harvesters. Finding some, he agreed to pay them
a pound a day, and the first squad began work. About 9 a.m.,
coming on some idle men in the market-place, the employer bade
them join the first lot, promising them a 'fair wage'. So they
too got down to work. At noon, and again at 3 p.m., he did
likewise. Then, about 5 p.m., an hour before sunset, meeting
some more unemployed, he said, 'Go and join the others in my
vineyard.'

But the really surprising thing happened one hour later when
falling darkness put an end to labour. The Jewish Law laid it
down, 'You shall not keep back a hired man's wages till next
morning.' So the employer said to his manager, 'Call the workers

24

together and pay them their wages, beginning with the last arrivals and ending with the first.'

When the last-comers stepped forward, though all they were entitled to was about eight pence, each got a pound in his hand, that is, the full day's wage. But, looking on, were the first-comers who had begun work at the break of day; and, when they saw what the later-comers got, and then themselves received the same amount, they were furious. 'These lay-abouts,' they protested, 'have worked only one hour, and yet you have put them on the same level as us who have been sweating it out in the heat of the sun since dawn. Is this what you call justice?'

It is the kind of protest any good trade-unionist would make today. 'Look, friend,' said the employer to the chief protester, 'I am not cheating you. Did we not agree on a pound a day? Well, you have got it. Off with you! If it is my pleasure to pay the last-comers the same as you, am I not free to do as I will with what is my own? Or are you jealous because I am kind?'

II

So we come back to our question, 'Was Jesus really discussing the problem of the just wage?'

He was not. He was answering those 'goody-goody' Jews, the Pharisees, who imagined that their piety entitled them to a special claim on God's reward and were shocked to see Jesus admitting all those 'bad characters' into God's Kingdom. For the crux of the whole story comes with that settlement at sunset and the astonishing generosity of the employer to the late-comers, i.e., the publicans and sinners.

This is not the parable of the Labourers in the Vineyard, as our forefathers named it. It is the parable of the Good Employer. He is the chief character in the story, and the Good Employer is God.

Jesus, in the story, is not talking about equal pay for equal work. He is talking theology, not economics. 'The rewards of God's Kingdom,' he is saying, 'are measured not by men's deserts but by their needs. God treats sinners as the good employer treated those unemployed men. This is what the heavenly Father is like; and, because he is like this, and acts like this, so do I.'

25

III

The man who told this story knew God better than any other ever born of woman, and what he tells us is as true today as it was then. God is like the good employer. In an earthly family a good father gives according to his children's needs, not according to their deserts. So it is in that great kingdom over which God rules as father.

But (someone may object) is not the story irrelevant and out of date because those Pharisees are long dead and buried? Are they indeed? Does not every age throw up people like them? Did not Robert Burns have to contend with them in eighteenth-century Ayrshire? Or have we forgotten how many pious Christians criticized John Wesley for taking the Gospel to the 'sinners' of his day – the colliers, weavers, and day-labourers whom he won for Christ? Or have we forgotten how conventional and well-to-do Christians sneered at William Booth for offering 'soup, soap and salvation' to the East-Enders of London? Does not every generation produce its unlovely crop of self-righteous Christians who would make a 'closed shop' of God's Kingdom and try to exclude all who do not measure up to their standards?

The parable of the Good Employer makes certain things quite clear.

It reminds us all how fortunate it is for us that God does not deal with us on the basis of strict justice. Was not this Portia's plea to Shylock in *The Merchant of Venice*?

> Though justice be thy plea, consider this:
> That in the course of justice none of us
> Should see salvation. We do pray for mercy.

Christ's parable declares that God's thoughts are not our thoughts, nor his ways our ways, for 'the love of God is broader than the measure of man's mind'.

Moreover, it tells us that there is an equal reward for all in God's Kingdom. Does this shock us? An equal reward for the poorest and least worthy of Christ's disciples along with great Christians like Paul and Augustine, with Francis and Luther, with Wesley and Livingstone, with Albert Schweitzer and Dietrich Bonhoeffer, with Mary Slessor of Calabar and Mother Teresa of

Calcutta? It doesn't make sense, and it doesn't sound fair; but it is the will of God, and it is very wonderful. This, says our Lord to us, is what God is like. And if he is like this, how dare we be jealous? On the contrary, is not Christ saying to us in this great parable what he says more plainly in his Sermon on the Mount, 'There must be no limit to your goodness, as your heavenly Father's goodness knows no bounds'?

7

The Good Samaritan

(Luke 10.25–37)

A parable, said P. G. Wodehouse, is a Bible story which at first
sounds like a pleasant yarn, but keeps something up its sleeve
which suddenly pops up and leaves you flat. As 'flat' as that
'lawyer' must have felt who inspired Christ's story about the Good
Samaritan.

'The lawyer', observe, was not what we mean by the word. He
was a 'doctor of the Law', an expert in the Law of Moses: and, in
order to understand the exchanges between him and Jesus, we
should know that long before this the Jewish rabbis had summed
up the whole Law by putting together two commands from the
Pentateuch: first, Deuteronomy 6.5, 'You shall love the Lord
your God with all your heart', and, second, Leviticus 19.18: 'You
shall love your neighbour as yourself.'

So, when the lawyer 'tested' Jesus with the question, 'Master,
what shall I do to inherit eternal life?', it was not because he
longed to know the answer – he knew it already – but because he
wished to cross-examine Jesus as an authority on the Law.

Little did the examiner guess how he himself was about to be
examined!

The Jews, you should note, regarded the word 'neighbour' as
a term of limited liability. They could never admit that, when
their Law told them to 'love their neighbour', the word included
dogs of Gentiles or half-breeds like Samaritans.

When therefore our lawyer asked Jesus, 'What must I do to
inherit eternal life?', Jesus answered him with another question,
'What is the Law's answer?' Replied the lawyer: 'You shall love
the Lord your God with all your heart and your neighbour as

yourself.' 'Right answer,' responded Jesus, 'Do this, and you will live,' that is, have eternal life.

It was then that the lawyer felt emboldened to put the question he was really spoiling to ask Jesus: 'And who, pray, is my neighbour?'

What the man wanted was a theological debate. Jesus declined the invitation. Instead, he told a story not to answer the lawyer's question, but to show him that his was the wrong question. The right question is not, 'Whom may I regard as my neighbour?' but 'To whom can I be a neighbour?' And the right answer to this is: 'Any human being who needs my help.'

II

Now to the story. First, we see the lone traveller making his way along the so-called 'Path of Blood', those seventeen miles of dangerous road that slope down from Jerusalem to Jericho. Suddenly the robbers appear from nowhere, beat up their man, like many a modern 'mugger', strip him of his valuables, and vanish as quickly as they came. A little later, along come two pillars of the Jewish church – a priest and one of the minor clergy called a Levite. They cannot help seeing the wounded man by the roadside, but not a finger do they lift to help him. Perhaps they feared the robbers might re-appear and 'clobber' them too. Perhaps they were afraid that, if they stayed to help, they might be late for their sacred duties in the Temple. What we do know is that, human nature being what it is, we can often find reasons for evading a distasteful duty when we are faced by it. So off go priest and Levite on their famous wide detour: 'they passed by on the other side.'

Then along comes the hero of the story, and of all people he is one of those hated Samaritans – a half-breed heretic with whom no self-respecting Jew would have anything to do, for 'the Jews have no dealings with Samaritans'.

One look at the victim suffices. Dismounting, the Samaritan applies 'first aid', wine and oil to disinfect the wounds, with bandages to bind them up. Then, hoisting the man on his own beast, off he sets for the nearest hostelry to care for the man that night. Next morning he produces what in our money would be the equivalent of two ten pound notes. 'Look after him,' he says to the hotel-keeper,' and if you have to spend any more on him, I will reimburse you on my way back.'

The story told, Jesus asks the final question: 'Which of these three, my friend, proved neighbour to the man who fell among the robbers?' The lawyer returns the only possible answer, 'Why, the man who showed kindness to him.' 'Then,' said Jesus, 'Go and do as he did.'

III

With the exception of the Prodigal Son, no story told by Jesus has so left its mark on our language and thought. Nowadays we even have noble people known as 'The Telephone Samaritans' whose aim is to help those in dire distress of mind or body. But am I wrong in supposing that for many of us the parable is the story of the man who did his good deed? Is not this to miss the point that our Lord was making, namely, that our neighbour may well be the man we least expect? 'How can I love my neighbour if I don't know who he is?', said the lawyer. Jesus answered: 'Real love never asks questions like this. It knows no bounds of race. All it asks for is opportunities of going into action.'

When you think of the parable this way, does it not cease to be just the story of the man who did his good deed and become a damning indictment of all racial and religious superiority?

'Who is my neighbour?' To that question Christ still answers today, 'Wrong question. The right question is, To whom can I be a neighbour?' But he does not stop there. To all of us who call ourselves his followers he says: 'Go and do what that Samaritan did to all the unfortunates, whatever their creed or colour, who meet you on life's "Path of Blood".'

IV

One further point. In the early church it was customary to identify the Good Samaritan with our Lord himself. Today, with our better understanding of the parables, we recognize that this is bad *exegesis*, or biblical interpretation. A parable is not an allegory, to be decoded point by point. It makes one main point, and the details in it are like the feathers which wing the arrow to its mark.

30

But, if this old interpretation is not *exegetically* right, is it not *evangelically* true? For did not the teller of the parable himself become the Good Samaritan of us all when, by his cross, he brought us healing for our hurt and life by his death? If this is true – and it is the heart of the Gospel – are not you and I under obligation to honour and serve the hidden Christ who meets us (as he tells us in his parable about the Last Judgment) in all his stricken brothers?

If you visit the Holy Land today, your guide may point out to you 'the Inn of the Good Samaritan' on the Jericho Road. But the Jericho Road is not now merely in Israel; it is everywhere. Sooner or later, you and I find ourselves on it, and confronted by a wounded brother or sister. And to us, as to the lawyer, comes the command of Christ, 'Go and do as he did.'

8

The Last Judgment

(Matt. 25.31–46)

'You seem, sir,' said the Oxford lady to Dr Samuel Johnson in an
hour when the fear of death and judgment lay heavy upon him,
'You seem to forget the merits of our Redeemer.' 'Madam,' replied the honest old man, 'I do not forget the merits of my
Redeemer; but my Redeemer has said that he will set some on his
right hand and some on his left.'

What haunted Johnson's mind was Christ's parable of the Last
Judgment, which is one of the chief glories of St Matthew's
Gospel. But modern man, for the most part, no longer shares Dr
Johnson's fear. Having largely lost his belief in a living and judging God, he has lost with it the feeling of guilt – that painful sense
of accountability and self-contempt which follows when we have
done wrong.

Our trouble today is moral anaemia. Modern man is not
bothering about what his forefathers called 'sins'. For him, sins
have become amiable weaknesses, not crimes against a God who
'is of purer eyes than to behold iniquity'. So he tends to shuffle out
of personal responsibility for his misdeeds, pleading perhaps,
'Something came over me when I did it', and inviting the psycho-
logist to explain what that 'something' was. Moreover, if many
people today have any philosophy of life at all, it is the old pagan
one of 'Let us eat, drink and be merry, for tomorrow we die', and
there's an end to it all. Small wonder then that they lose no sleep
over Christ's teaching about a final judgment.

Such complacency is not open to us who call Christ Saviour
and Lord. As we believe in a living and righteous God, holding
with Christ that we are responsible to him for what we do in this
life, and that death does not finally settle all scores, we cannot

dismiss the doctrine of a Last Judgment as an outworn 'myth'. No doubt our godly forefathers to whom 'the great white throne' was not a 'grand perhaps' but a solemnizing certainty, painted the Last Judgment in lurid colours no longer credible by Christian men today. Yet no creed can be called truly Christian which does not affirm that hereafter we will be held accountable for what we have done, or failed to do, in this life.

II

So let us turn to the parable of the Last Judgment. 'When the Son of man comes in glory,' it begins, 'he will sit in state on his throne with all the nations gathered before him.' The reference is plainly to the consummation of God's Kingdom at the end of time when the human race, reaching its last frontier post, will encounter, not nothingness but God in Christ. Who then is to be our judge at God's great assize? The answer is that 'the Son of man', who later in the parable is called 'the King', can only be Christ himself. As Studdert-Kennedy, better known as 'Woodbine Willie', phrased it in his vivid way:

> Then will he come, with meekness for his glory,
> God in a workman's jacket as before,
> Living again the eternal Gospel story,
> Sweeping the shavings from his workshop floor.

The second question is: who are the people here standing before his judgment seat? Who are the subjects of the judgment? Our scholars agree that 'all the nations' here must mean the Gentiles, that is, the heathen world. Here then we have our Lord's answer to the question, 'By what criterion will those heathen men be judged who have never known you?' 'The heathen,' he replies, 'have met me in my brethren, for all the poor and needy ones are my brothers. Therefore, on the great day, they will be judged by the compassionate love they have shown to the afflicted, in whom they have met me incognito; and if they have fulfilled the royal law of love, they will share in my Father's heavenly kingdom.'

Thus, the 'justification' at the last day of those who have not known Christ will be a justification by love. And, if there is for

33

others condemnation, then, by the same token, it will be for lack of love to men and women in their miseries.

Someone has called this parable 'the story of the great surprises': on the one hand, the surprise of 'the blessed ones' who had 'stumbled into Paradise', all unware that in helping the needy, they had been confronting Christ himself; and, on the other hand, the surprise of the condemned ones who would (they implied) have acted so very differently had they but known that these poor unfriended ones were indeed Christ's brothers.

III

What word of God then does this remarkable parable carry for us today?

Does it not teach us that in Christ's view among the most grievous of all sins is inhumanity to our fellow men, and that, 'though now ascended up on high', he still cares utterly for all the hungry, the ill-clad, the outcasts and the prisoners? Does it not face us Christians today with the question, What are we doing now to help the poor, the ill-fed and the afflicted folk whom Christ calls his brothers? Rightly did Dietrich Bonhoeffer, greatest of modern martyrs, declare, 'The church is her true self *only when she exists for others.*' As God has cared for us in Christ, so we are in turn called to care for all his afflicted children in whom Christ hiddenly confronts us today.

Turgenev, the Russian novelist, tells how once, as he worshipped with peasants in a simple country church, a man came up and stood by him who, he felt, must be Christ himself. But he had a face like all men's faces. 'What sort of Christ is this?', he asked himself. 'Such an ordinary, ordinary man. It cannot be.' In vain he strove to resist his first impression. He could not. Then at last the truth came home to him. 'Only then I realized,' he said, 'that just such a face – a face like all men's faces – is the face of Christ.'

Just so, with 'a face like all men's faces', the hidden Christ confronts us still, confronts us in the persons of all who stand in need of our help and succour. If we lightly turn away and shut our ears against their crying need, we may be rejecting Christ himself. It is a solemnizing thought. Listen:

34

He that careth for a wounded brother
Watcheth not alone;
There are three in the darkness together,
And the third is the Lord.

Happy the man who thus finds Christ!

9

Keep Knocking!

(Luke 11.5–8; 18.2–8)

Our Lord Jesus had an unforgettable way of arguing from the human to the divine. For him, God was holy, but he was not, as some modern theologians have held, 'wholly other'. He believed earthly analogies could figure forth to men God's nature and will. Human experience was for him a kind of springboard for the adventure of faith. He had a way of saying, 'Take the very best you know among humans. God is all that – and incomparably more!' So, starting from human values, he invited his disciples to project them into the unseen world, and see in them a reflection of the invisible God, the maker of heaven and earth. For an example, listen to him teaching his disciples:

> Is there a man among you who will offer his son a stone when he asks for bread, or a snake when he asks for fish? If you then, bad as you are, know how to give your children what is good for them, how much more will your heavenly Father give good things to those who ask him?

So Jesus encouraged his men to believe in God the Father Almighty – to believe in 'the humanity of God'. Now, as theology is simply 'faith thinking', faith giving a reasoned account of itself, so prayer is simply *faith in action*. Our Lord never defined prayer, as, for example, *The Shorter Catechism* does; he did better – he gave his disciples a pattern prayer, and in his parables bade them 'expect great things from God'.

Take this one from the eleventh chapter of Luke's Gospel. Traditionally known as 'the Friend at Midnight', it would be much better named 'the Grumpy Neighbour'.

Late one night a hungry traveller turned up unexpectedly at a

36

friend's house and caught him without a bit of bread in his cupboard. The only thing the householder could do was to knock up a neighbour and ask him for three loaves – the usual meal for one person. And very politely he did, explaining why he had to.

Now peep into the single-roomed house of that sleeping neighbour. There are his children bedded down on a raised mat, with the parents one at each end, when suddenly at midnight comes a loud hammering on the door! The head of the house, rudely awoken from his slumbers, is not amused. 'Don't be a confounded nuisance,' he growls to the knocker outside. 'My door was locked hours ago. If I get up, I'll disturb the whole family.'

But outside in the darkness our hero refuses to take no for an answer. On he keeps knocking until at last, in sheer desperation, the grumpy neighbour gets up, unbolts the door, and hands over the three loaves.

Now Jesus is talking to his disciples about prayer. 'If a human friend,' he is saying, 'can be induced to get up and give help, how much more will God your heavenly Father – and perfect Friend – be ready to supply your needs!'

This is what believing prayer is like. The disciple with a faith like this will open his heart freely to the great unseen Father, sure that he will hear him. He will also be able to accept whatever God sends, believing that the all-wise Father above knows his children's needs better than they do themselves.

Seven chapters later in St Luke's Gospel, we find what may be called the twin of this parable. Traditionally known as 'the Importunate Widow', it might better be named 'the Callous Judge'.

This time the scene is a law-court, with the plaintiff a poor widow woman whose opponent has refused to settle a lawful debt. So, time after time, she keeps coming before the judge and crying, 'Give me justice!' But the judge, by his own confession, 'fears neither God nor man' – is swayed neither by religious principle nor by public opinion. At first he does nothing. After all, she is only a helpless widow, without money or influence. Why bother? No doubt when she started up in court, he called out 'Next case, please!'

But, if the judge could keep on, so could the widow. Day after

37

day back she came to plague him, until at last he relented and gave her what she sought. 'Maybe I don't give a damn for God or man,' we can almost hear him saying, 'yet because this tiresome widow keeps pestering me, I will give her justice.' And he did.

Now, observe, Jesus is not here offering the judge and his behaviour as a picture of what God is like. He is not describing God as some ungracious deity who needs to be badgered into compliance. He is saying, in effect: 'If even this curmudgeonly judge could be moved to act by the widow's persistence, how much more will God answer his people's prayers for vindication!'

What these two parables of Jesus show, as indeed his whole life shows, is how constantly he leaned on God his heavenly Father, believing in the power of prayer, because he knew what kind of being the great hearer of prayer was – and is.

Is not our Lord today calling his followers to such prayer?

'Prayer,' wrote P. T. Forsyth,' is for our religious life what original research is for the scientist.' Why? Because by it, he explained, we make contact with reality – with the last Reality in the universe. And in one of his books he records, 'I saw in a friend's house a picture by Dürer, the great German painter. It was just two hands, palms together, and lifted in prayer. I wish (he went on) I could stamp that picture on the page of my book and fit to it John Milton's phrase – "the great two-handed engine at our door".'

Then why, O why, in these troubled times, don't we Christians make more use of that 'great two-handed engine'?

Do we think ourselves wiser than our Lord, or indeed poets, prophets and even politicians down the centuries?

It was Abraham Lincoln, greatest of all Americans, who declared, 'I have been driven many times to my knees by the overwhelming conviction that I had nowhere else to go. My own wisdom and that of all around me seemed insufficient for the day.' It was Alfred Lord Tennyson who wrote: 'More things are wrought by prayer than this world dreams of.' And a greater than Lincoln or Tennyson who assured his disciples, as he still assures us:

Ask, and it shall be given you,
Seek, and you will find,
Knock, and it will be opened to you.

So, Christian friends, keep knocking! It is not my command but our Lord's. So I will say it again, 'Keep knocking!'

10

'Pray then like this'

(Matt. 6.9 RSV)

In his diary for 1 March 1939, Edwin Muir, the Scottish poet, described how he underwent a kind of 'conversion' by reciting the Lord's Prayer as he took off his waistcoat before going to bed. He was (he wrote) 'overcome by joyful surprise' when he realized that everything in the prayer, apart from the Being to whom it is addressed, refers to human life, seen realistically and not mystically, and is about the world and society, and not just about the everlasting destiny of the human soul.

Would it not be a good thing for some of us church people if we could undergo a like 'conversion'? Every Sunday we repeat the prayer, yet so familiar are its words that we seldom stop to think what they mean, and they tend to become just a piece of holy patter. (Might we not, in fact, before we repeat it, say, 'From pattered Paternosters deliver us, good Lord'?)

Here, then, let us take another look at the prayer and see if we can understand it better.

I

St Luke tells us that it all began with a request from Christ's disciples: 'Lord, teach us how to pray, as John taught his disciples' (Luke 11.1). 'Pray then like this,' he answered, and gave them the pattern prayer. .

Its plan is simplicity itself. At the beginning an invocation (or address to God); at the end, a doxology (or ascription of praise) and, in between, six petitions. Three are for the greater glory of God in the world, and three are for our human needs.

'Our Father who art in heaven,' it begins. 'Who art in heaven' is not just a pointer to the place of God's abode but a reminder

40

that if God is a Father, he is (to quote the *Te Deum*) 'the Father of an infinite majesty', to be approached by us with reverence.

For any religion the supreme question is, 'What is God like?' And for Christians there is only one right answer: 'God is a heavenly Father.' It was Christ's way to say to his disciples (as in his parable about the Asking Son (Matt. 7.9–11): 'Think of the very best human father you can imagine – God is all that – and how much more!) Great and holy beyond all our conceiving, but a Father – a Father who cares for his children, who is sad when they go astray and glad when, like the prodigal son, they come home, a Father to whom his own life was one long obedience, and to whom at last, as he hung on the cross, he commended his spirit.

This is the God we address as 'our Father'. Note the word 'our'. When we say it, we join ourselves with the whole family of God on earth, for this is the prayer 'that spans the world'.

The first petition says: 'Hallowed be thy name.' Sometimes we say airily, 'What's in a name?' For us, a 'name' is often little more than a tag for the postman's convenience. The Bible takes names more seriously. In the Bible the 'name' stands for a person's *nature* (or character), so that God's 'name' is his nature as he reveals it.

Now God has revealed his nature to us in various ways – in his creation (see Psalm 19.1–6), in his dealings in history with his people Israel, but, above all, as 'Abba, Father' in Christ his well-beloved Son. So, when we pray 'hallowed be thy name', we pray that God may everywhere be worshipped and obeyed as our heavenly Father.

The second petition says: 'Thy Kingdom come!' What does the Kingdom of God mean? Not, as some have supposed, some welfare state, under divine auspices, to be built by human hands. God's kingdom (*basileia*) means God's reign, God acting in his sovereign power. It is God the Father in his royal grace entering history in order to save his people from their sins and woes.

More, it is the very heart of the Gospel, or 'Good News', that God's reign began decisively when he sent his Son to reconcile a sinful world to himself (II Cor. 5.19).

Yet this was only a beginning, and from it, Christ said, would

41

come a great ending – or consummation. This is what we commonly mean by the phrase 'Kingdom come'. So, in the second petition, we pray God to consummate, or complete, the salvation he began when he sent Christ as Saviour.

In that 'Kingdom come' all the promises of the Beatitudes will come true. Then the mourners will be comforted, the merciful will obtain mercy, the pure in heart will see God, and his redeemed children will be for ever at home in their Father's house.

Only God can consummate this saving rule of his. Does this mean that we men are to sit back idly with folded arms and wait for it? On the contrary, 'Thy will be done on earth as it is done in heaven,' says the third petition. Is it not a summons to God's servants to be up and doing: 'Thy will be done – and done by me!'?

But (you say) what is God's will? It is what pleases God. And what this is, Christ tells us in the Sermon on the Mount (Matt. 5–7) and elsewhere. It is loving, not hating; giving, not grabbing; the Golden Rule (Matt. 7.12) and not the rule of the jungle ('devil take the hindmost'). In God's heaven it is always so, and here we pray that in this respect earth may become more like heaven.

II

So ends the first half of the prayer. Having asked for the 'heavenly' things, we are free now to pray for the 'earthly' ones, i.e., for our human needs, and, in particular, for three things: provision, pardon and protection. 'Give,' 'forgive', and, finally, 'deliver', is what Christ bids us say.

First, 'give us this day our daily bread'. This petition teaches our dependence on God. Sometimes we say of a man that he has 'independent means'. But none of us really has. We cannot command the harvest, and all our tractors and combine harvesters would be so much useless metal if God did not quicken life within the seed. Ultimately, our daily bread comes not from the farmer, not from the miller, but from the Creator. And this our dependence on his bounty we acknowledge whenever we say grace before meat.

Here notice that Christ authorizes us to ask only for what we really need. It is a prayer for daily bread – for the staff of life –

42

and not for daily cake, still less caviar! Moreover, this petition does not rule out the human effort required to make God's gift our own. As a wise old Scots woman once put it – and it goes for us as well as for the wild birds – 'God feeds the sparrows, but he doesn't push the crumbs into their mouths.'

Come now to the fifth petition: 'And forgive us our debts as we forgive (or, more accurately, "have forgiven") our debtors.'

From bread we turn to sin. For there is another hunger – the soul's hunger for forgiveness of all the sins that separate us from holy God. 'Debts' here is a metaphor for 'sins' – for all the wrongs we have done and all the good we have left undone. But mark the words: 'as we have forgiven our debtors.' Christ tell us solemnly that we need not look for God's forgiveness if we are not ready to forgive our offending brother (Matt. 6.14f.). 'Forgive,' he says, 'as you hope to be forgiven.' 'For,' as Lord Tennyson paraphrased his words:

> For all the blessèd saints in heaven
> Are both forgivers and forgiven.

So to the last petition: 'And lead us not into temptation but deliver us from evil' (or, 'from the evil one').

Here 'temptation' does not mean enticement to evil. The good God never so entices (James 1.13). 'Temptation' here means 'testing', and without 'testing' we should never develop any moral muscle or backbone. Yet, by the same token, every such 'testing' involves the risk that we may succumb to the fatal downward pull of evil. So, in this last petition, we pray: 'Lord, spare us dangerous moral adventures, but, when they do befall us, help us to come safely through them.'

Then, as with a peal of trumpets, the prayer ends with the doxology.

Such is our Lord's Prayer, the prayer he taught his disciples, the prayer that teaches how to pray. Still today it remains the Christian's prayer, the prayer he ought to pray every day – every day and with 'all that in him is'.

43

II

The Acted Parables of Christ

(Mark 9.36; John 13.4; Mark 14.22)

Actions, they say, speak louder than words. A simple act, innocent of any speech, will often speak more movingly than a multitude of words. Goethe, the great German, went further. 'The highest,' he said, 'cannot be spoken, it can only be acted.' The prophets of Israel were of much the same opinion. When words no longer availed, they resorted to symbolic actions, in order to declare God's will. Thus, Jeremiah, foretelling disaster for his nation, once shattered an earthenware jar before his countrymen, as if to say, 'As it happens to this jar, so it is about to happen to Jerusalem when God judges his faithless people.'

In a similar way our Lord himself sometimes chose to preach and teach God's truth by actions rather than by words. Let us take three examples from the gospels.

I

First, 'he took a child'.

A child. Not an eagle, not a lion, but a little child, whom he set among his disciples.

Christ's regard for children is of course writ large in the gospel story. How he watched them playing at their marriages and funerals in the market place! How his indignation blazed out at his disciples for belittling them! How pleased he was with their praises when all others seemed to be turning against him! Now this regard for little children is one of the unique traits in our Lord. You may search the literature of antiquity from end to end, and you will not find its like. Nevertheless, for Christ, the little child, precious indeed in his own right, was something more. Listen to what he says: 'Whosoever shall not receive the Kingdom

44

of God as a little child, he shall not enter therein.' For Christ, the child was a living symbol of the kind of character needed for God's Kingdom.

Was it then the innocence of the little child that he had in mind? It was not. Christ came to save sinners, not innocents. Moreover, whatever doting parents may say, little children are not always little innocents – ask any nursemaid! No, here it is of the child's relation to its parents Christ is thinking. On them the child depends entirely. Everything comes from them – is their gift. Not the innocence of the child but its *receptiveness* is what Christ desiderates in his disciples. Unless we are ready to receive God's Kingdom as a child takes a present from his parent's hands, we shall not have it.

'Whosoever shall not receive the Kingdom of God as a little child . . .' It is still true. Men still enter God's Kingdom in the same way. The Kingdom of our Father is not for the proud or the self-sufficient – the men who imagine that they are righteous and can save themselves. Still it belongs to the humble of heart who, confessing their weakness and owning their sinfulness, cast themselves on the forgiving grace of God in Jesus Christ, his saviour Son.

II

'He took a towel.'

Do you recall the scene of this acted parable? It was the upper room, on the night before the crucifixion. The supper had begun – that supper to which all our Lord's Suppers run back – when suddenly (Luke tells us), contention flared up among the twelve disciples. Think of it – Jesus their Master soon going out to the agony in Gethsemane and the cross, and his disciples are still quarrelling about who was to be the greatest – still blinded by visions of thrones and crowns! Could anything that Jesus might say pierce the darkness in their minds? No, but his act will speak to them, speak to them more powerfully than any word. Silently, Jesus procures a towel and a basin, puts off his coat, and is down upon his knees washing his disciples' feet. The Son of God has become a servant – the Servant of the Lord.

With his towel and basin, he goes round them all, one by one,

45

including Judas who will soon be slipping out into the darkness to finish his black treachery. Now he moves round to Peter, who at first demurs indignantly, 'You, Lord, washing my feet!', only to be told, 'If I do not wash your feet, you are not in fellowship with me.'

The acted parable over, Jesus, taking his garments, goes again to the head of the table. 'If I have washed your feet,' he says, 'you also ought to wash one another's feet, for I have given you an example.'

What does this mean for us? That we who are his latter-day disciples should literally repeat his action? No, this would be to confuse the letter with the spirit. The example Christ set them, as he sets us today, is one of lowly service to others. Our Lord's taking of the towel, his donning of the slave's apron, proclaimed in a way that words could not, that what had formerly been the badge of slavery was to be henceforth the badge of the highest and holiest service, the badge of the only kingdom which is divine:

> Its King a Servant, and its sign
> A gibbet on a hill.

Not crowns and coronets but towels and basins are the insignia of that kingdom, and he best honours the Son of God who is prepared to stoop and serve.

III

'He took a loaf.'

The third, the last, the greatest of his acted parables, and one that has reverberated down the centuries and round the world.

Again, the background is the upper room on the night in which he was betrayed, as once again Christ chooses one of earth's commonest things to teach his heavenly truth. Only a loaf of bread, we sometimes say. Ah, but this is to think too meanly of bread. For, besides being 'the staff of life', the mere eating together of bread has been from time immemorial the symbol of friendship. When therefore Christ 'took a loaf', was he simply preaching an action sermon on the golden text of friendship? Far from it! 'This is my body broken for you,' he told his disciples. 'As it happens to this loaf, so it is happening to me.' It

46

is this word of his over the loaf which puts atonement into what happened, not long after, outside a city wall. 'Take, eat,' he commanded his disciples, and the eating which followed was more than a simple sequel to his acted parable. It was nothing less than the gift to them of 'a share in the power of the broken Christ' – a share in the virtue of his saving death. It is as if Christ were saying, 'Eating this broken bread, you are entering into God's redeeming purpose. You are making your own all that my Father is doing through me for men's salvation.'

Even so, nineteen centuries later, as Christ's disciples, we take and eat. No more than the first disciples may we fathom all the deep mysteries of the Saviour's passion, for:

> None of the ransomed ever knew
> How deep were the waters crossed.

But their Lord is our Lord, now reigning in heaven whence, through the Holy Spirit, he is present with us, unseen but not unknown. We believe that he was 'broken' for us; that, as we fulfil his command, 'This do for my recalling', he still comes to be the meat and drink of our souls, and that he is able to save to the uttermost all who come to God through him:

> And so we come: O draw us to thy feet,
> Most patient Saviour, who canst love us still,
> And by this food, so awful and so sweet,
> Deliver us from every touch of ill:
> In thine own service make us glad and free,
> And grant us nevermore to part with thee.

12

The Clemency of Christ

(John 8.1–11 AV)

In the second century AD there circulated, orally, in the Syrian church a remarkable story about Jesus and a woman who had been caught in adultery. Some Christian scholars, whose duty it was to copy the four gospels, evidently thought it ought to have a place in them. But where? Some put it where it now stands in our Authorized Version, in the eighth chapter of John's Gospel, thinking that it illustrated Christ's words in that chapter, 'I judge no man' (John 8.15). But other scribes, with much better insight, inserted the story in the twenty-first chapter of Luke's Gospel where, near the end of his ministry, Jesus is described as teaching in the Temple at Jerusalem (Luke 21.37).

If you turn up The New English Bible, you will find that 'the story has been relegated to an appendix at the end of John's Gospel. Some may think this rather shoddy treatment for a story about Jesus which has all the marks of authenticity upon it – betrays 'the Christ touch'. Like the story about the tribute money, our tale almost certainly belongs to the final phase of Christ's earthly ministry when his enemies in Jerusalem were trying to trap him into some fatal admission and so compass his downfall and death.

So let us study the story in some detail.

I

The first point to note is that this is the only occasion in the gospels where we read of Jesus writing – writing not, however, with a pen on paper but with his finger on the ground. Why, and what, was he writing?

Some have suggested that he was scribbling, almost mechanically, on the ground, to cover his embarrassment at the whole sorry spectacle confronting him. He was 'doodling', as we say nowadays, in order to conceal his sense of shame at sin being made an excuse by so-called religious men, in order to further their own dark designs.

Another suggestion is that the Greek verb used here should be translated 'registered' and that 'ground' means 'dust'. Jesus was 'registering' the accusation of the Scribes and the Pharisees 'in the dust', so that there might be no permanent record of it.

But the likeliest explanation – which we owe to the late Professor T. W. Manson – is that which makes Jesus play the part of a Roman judge.

Like the tribute money, this is the tale of a trap set for Jesus by his enemies. If he sanctions the stoning of the adulteress, he is usurping the power of Rome who alone could inflict capital punishment. If he forbids it, he is breaking the law of Moses which demanded death for an adulteress (Lev. 20.10). But, again, Jesus adroitly avoids the trap set for him – this time by writing with his finger on the ground.

Now this writing accorded with the procedures of Roman law. In a Roman court the sitting judge would first write down the sentence on a tablet, before getting up and reading it aloud. This is what Jesus did. By his action he was saying in effect, 'You are inviting me to play the judge in true Roman fashion. Very well, I will do so.' Stooping down, he pretends to write the sentence on the ground, after which he straightens up and reads it out: 'Let him who is without sin be the first to throw a stone at her.' ('The first stones shall be thrown by the witnesses' of the deed meriting the death sentence, said the Law of Moses. See Deut. 17.1.)

Thus our Lord defeats the plotters by 'going through the motions' of passing sentence on the woman, but at the same time so wording it that it cannot be carried out. He does not condone the woman's sin – 'Go and sin no more,' he says – but neither does he condemn her. What we have here is not a formal acquittal: it is a refusal to judge, in perfect agreement with one who said in his Sermon on the Mount, 'Judge not, that you be not judged.'

49

Now turn from the Lord to his apostle. Twice in his letters to his converts, St Paul bids them show 'magnanimity' like Christ's (II Cor. 1.10 and Phil. 4.5 NEB). 'Magnanimity', from the Latin *magnus* 'big' and *animus* 'mind', means literally 'big-mindedness'. The magnanimous man is the one who knows how to relax justice and let mercy come in. And does not Christ's treatment of the adulteress, with its delicate balancing of justice and mercy, perfectly exemplify it?

I can think of no better commentary on Christ's magnanimity as exhibited in the story of the adulteress than the words of Portia to the Jew Shylock in Shakespeare's *The Merchant of Venice*:

> The quality of mercy is not strain'd,
> It droppeth as the gentle rain from heaven
> Upon the place beneath; it is twice bless'd,
> It blesseth him that gives and him that takes . . .
> It is an attribute of God himself,
> And earthly power doth then show likest God's
> When mercy seasons justice.

Mercy, like that of God himself, 'mercy seasoning justice', as Shakespeare defines it, is what the story of Jesus and the adulteress is all about.

Do you remember Burns's counsel in his 'Address to the Unco Guid':

> Then gently scan your brother man,
>   Still gentler sister woman;
> Tho' they may gang a kennin wrang
>   To step aside is human?

But is not such 'stepping aside' – this 'magnanimity' – more than merely human? Is it not, as Shakespeare says, truly 'divine'? And are we not called as Christians to 'have the same mind in us which was also in Christ Jesus' (Phil. 2.5)?

What then has the story of Jesus and the adulteress to say to us today? From time to time it falls to some of us Christians to sit in judgment on men and women who have sullied the sacred bond of marriage or sinned in similar sad ways. Should not the tale of Christ and the adulteress carry for us a plain reminder that the strictly legal application of laws, like the law of Moses, is not really the best way of dealing with sinners as persons, persons made in the image of God? More especially when we remember that not even the best of us is sinless?

13

'Consider the lilies'

(Matt. 6.28)

When, after long winter, there comes once again the annual miracle of spring and before our eyes is spread out all the wonder and bloom of the world, should not we Christians sometimes remind ourselves of what nature in all her aspects meant to Christ himself? It is one of the charms of the gospels that they never allow us to forget that we are living in a world where the grass grows green, the lilies bloom, and the birds sing. As the poet put it:

> Christ spoke of grass, and wind, and rain
> And fig-trees, and fair weather,
> And made it his delight to bring
> Heaven and earth together.

We need not wonder at this. Galilee was known as 'the garden of Palestine'. His own city, Nazareth, where Christ grew to manhood, commands from its hill-tops glorious views of that land in whose heart, like some blue gem, lies the Lake of Galilee. Small wonder then that the gospels abound with all the sights and sounds of nature, or that:

> When Christ walked the fields he drew
> From the flowers and birds and dew
> Parables of God.

I

Best-known of all his nature sayings is that about the lilies: 'Consider the lilies of the field how they grow; they toil not, neither do they spin; and yet I say unto you that even Solomon in all his glory was not arrayed like one of these.'

For Christ these 'lilies' (not daffodils but scarlet anemones and poppies which, because they were so abundant, the women used to burn as fuel in their ovens) were finer far than King Solomon in all his royal purple.

'Alive today, and tomorrow in the oven,' says Christ. It is an old motif, this of the transience of life on earth – 'the grass withers and the flower falls off.' But note how Christ gives it a new turn. For him, the lesson is: 'These things die, and so must we. But, if God lavishes such pains on these, brief though their life is, how much more will he care for us his children!'

Note, next, how Christ has brooded over the mystery of unfolding buds. 'First the blade,' he comments in his parable, 'then the ear, then the full corn in the ear.' No less has he watched the annual miracle of harvest. 'Lift up your eyes,' he says to his disciples, 'and look on the fields, for they are already white unto harvest.' He has studied the wild birds, and bids his over-anxious disciples take a lesson from them: 'Look at the birds of the air: they neither sow nor reap nor gather into barns, and yet your heavenly Father feeds them. Are you not of more value than they?' He has even spared a glance for the sparrow chirping in the roadway, the sparrow that men sold in the market for two a penny. 'Not one of them,' he says, 'falls to the ground without your Father.'

And then the sunshine and the rain! Christ bids us notice that God sends them to all men – good and evil, just and unjust. This is the great grace of the Creator. What a width of charity that must betoken in the heart of God! We keep our smiles for our friends, and reserve our scowls for our enemies. But God gives his favours to all alike, without distinction.

Even the beasts of the field claimed Christ's attention. Once, you may remember, he contrasted his own lot with theirs: 'Foxes have holes, and the birds of the air have nests, but the Son of man has nowhere to lay his head.' Think of it! He who now reigns in the highest place that heaven affords once found time to watch the fox stealing to his lair and the wild birds building in the hedgerows.

53

Nature, too, in her homelier aspects figures largely in the gospels. The life and work of the farmer Christ evidently knew well. He speaks of sowing: 'Behold, a sower went forth to sow,' he says in one of his parables in which he pictures God as the Great Sower. He speaks of ploughing: 'No man, having set his hand to the plough, and looking back, is fit for the Kingdom of God,' he warns a prospective disciple. He talks of lost sheep and of oxen that stumble into hidden holes. And one of his saddest similes is drawn from the life of the barnyard fowl. As he journeyed south to Jerusalem, the Jerusalem that was soon to spike him to a cross, a sob came into his voice as he cried, 'O Jerusalem, Jerusalem, who killest the prophets and stonest them who are sent unto thee, how often would I have gathered thy children together as a hen gathers her chickens under her wings – and you would not!'

II

Thus and thus did our Lord speak of nature. What did nature say to him?

No one who reads the psalmists and prophets or the book of Job can doubt what nature said to the men of the Old Testament. 'The heavens declare the glory of God and the firmament showeth his handiwork.' The voice of God they hear in nature is one of power and glory. When the storm rages, they say:

> The voice of the Lord breaketh the cedars,
> Yea, the Lord breaketh the cedars of Lebanon.

To the men of the Old Covenant nature spoke of the might and majesty of the living God, the great Creator and the Lord of history, who not only brings out the evening stars, but, sitting above the circle of the earth, controls the destiny of men and nations, who before him are as grasshoppers. In short, it is of the power and glory of God that his creation speaks to the men of old Israel.

But, when you move from the Old Testament to the New, you cannot but mark a difference. If you turn up the sixth chapter of St Matthew's Gospel – the middle part of the Sermon on the Mount – you will find there the word, no less than a dozen times, the word which makes all the difference. It is the word 'Father'.

What nature said to Christ was, 'Have faith in an almighty Father, the Lord of heaven and earth.' For him, the thought of God in all his power and glory was softened and blended in the thought of his Fatherhood. It was the Father's hand that had reared the hills. It was the Father's hand which was upon the storm, bidding it be still. At the back of the thunder, no less than in the lilies and the sparrows, was a Father's steadfast love.

Not that Christ was blind to what is terrible in nature, to nature 'red in tooth and claw', as Tennyson called it. He saw the wolves that devour the flock, the vultures that swoop down on the carcase. He knew the earthquake and the flood that could sweep away the sand-built house like a cockle shell. Yet these things did not shadow his perfect trust in God. Right through his whole life, from the time when as a boy he stood in the Temple to the time when upon the cross he committed his spirit to God, his was the faith that:

> This is my Father's world,
> O let me ne'er forget
> That though the wrong
> Seems oft so strong,
> God is its Ruler yet.

III

So nature spoke to Christ. What should it say to us who take his name upon us and call ourselves Christians?

We live in other times, and under other skies. Yet, still year by year, God spreads out before us the lovely sacrament of nature.

With Christ for teacher, when we look upon the lilies of our land, can we not hear God saying to us: 'I made these. These are my thoughts wrought out in living leaf and blade. Can you not see what beauty must dwell in the heart of him who made them?' As we watch the wild birds, can we not hear God saying, 'I care for these. Not one falls to the ground without my will or knowledge. Shall I not much more care for you who are of more value than many sparrows?'

And as we watch the corn grow and ripen for the bread – our 'daily bread' – can we not hear God saying, through that same bread now transfigured into a sacrament of his Son's sacrifice for our salvation – saying; 'I made you. I care for you. And I have redeemed you.'

So, in a common loaf, the doctrines of Creation, Providence, and Redemption are wonderfully conjoined; and from the sight of the waving cornfields – symbol of the Creator's providing care – we rise to the mystery of:

> The corn that makes the holy bread
> By which the soul of man is fed.

Consider, then, the lilies of the field, ponder well the Gospel that they preach, and let your prayer and mine be this:

> O Lord our God, teach us to know
> How beautifully lilies grow.
> Give us that faith in Thy good care
> Which lilies breathe in open air.
> Help us to keep our hearts as clean
> As lovely lilies, white and green.
> And, as they, low-laid in the ground,
> Relive again when Spring comes round,
> So may we, when life's day is fled,
> Rise like Thy lilies from the dead.

14

Taking us as we are

(Mark 10.38f.)

It is a comfort sometimes to remember that the first disciples of our Lord were not pillar saints, sprouting haloes, but, like ourselves, very human and fallible folk, each with his own quota of original sin.

For evidence we need look no further than this story about James and John, the two 'sons of thunder', as Jesus nicknamed them, probably because they were of an impetuous nature and liable to sound off like a thunderclap. (Once, we are told, they wanted to call down fire from heaven on a Samaritan village which had slammed its doors in Christ's face.)

It is the story of a thoroughly selfish request by two of Christ's closest disciples. James and John asked for nothing less than the chief places in Christ's coming messianic 'glory'. 'You do not know what you are asking,' he replied. 'Can you drink of the cup that I am drinking?' (He meant the cup of God's wrath against sin.) At once they responded, 'We can.' And Jesus took them at their word. 'This cup that I am drinking you shall drink,' he said, hinting at the suffering they would yet have to endure for his sake and the Gospel's. But he added that the gift of the chief places in his glory rested in higher hands than his.

James and John had no idea what they were asking. Yet Jesus took them at their word. What lay behind his acceptance of their brash and ignorant 'We can'? Why, this important truth that, if a master is going to do anything with his disciples, he must, to start with, *take them as they are*. If they pledge themselves in their own terms, provided that they are sincere, this is enough – for a beginning.

Let us dwell upon this truth, and, first of all, from the angle of the master.

I

Inevitably, there is always an element of cross-purpose between a leader and his followers. This it is which makes leadership such a difficult business. To be a leader, you must be ahead of your followers, yet not too far ahead. You must contrive to live in your own lonely world, and yet, at the same time in theirs.

Consider, then, how formidable was Christ's task in training his disciples, and how great was his wisdom that he succeeded in it. He succeeded in carrying his disciples over from their own little world, in which ambition was a ruling motive, into his own great world – the Kingdom of his Father – where ambition did not count. He succeeded in turning his all-too-human handful of men – each one, it has been said, capable of breaking his heart – into what the *Te Deum* calls 'the glorious company of the apostles'. And he succeeded because, to start with, he took them as they were.

There is food for thought here, in so far as you and I are called to be leaders in our day. The church of Christ professes, and holds out before its members, moral standards and ideals far ahead of the world's. Those of us who find ourselves leaders in it must avoid the error which so many persons with ideals make in their efforts to uplift the world. It is the mistake of going all 'spiritual highbrow' – of wanting to sweep people off at once into rarefied spiritual atmospheres to which they are quite unaccustomed.

For example: a man expresses a desire to join Christ's church. Some earnest, well-meaning Christian at once tells him that, if he does join, he must accept the Apostles' Creed, go to church every Sunday, read his ·Bible, and say his daily prayers. He refuses to join: he says it is too much. Wiser far if we asked him whether he could accept some short and simple statement of Christian belief like that which James Denney proposed for Christians: 'I believe in God through Jesus Christ his only Son, our Lord and Saviour,' and whether he was honestly resolved to lead a Christian life. That way you may make a convert; almost certainly you will not win him the other way. And if you think

58

it is a pretty small beginning, remember that we have in his parables Christ's own authority for believing that 'small beginnings can have great endings'.

II

Now consider the matter from the angle of the disciple. When James and John answered Jesus' challenge with their 'We can', there were two elements in their promise that need examining: one, an element of ignorance – they didn't know what they were asking; and, two, an element of wrong motive   they had their eye on the best places in Christ's coming glory. Yet Jesus took them as they were, because in that ignorant and wrong-motived assurance of theirs, he discerned the possibility of greater things.

Consider, first, the element of ignorance, for it concerns us also. Many people refuse their allegiance to Christ because they fear that, if they promise to follow him, they will not be able to keep to their promise. 'If I make a promise,' they explain, 'I like to keep it, and rather than not keep it, I won't make it.'

Honesty? Yes, but honesty of rather a myopic sort. Better far to say, 'I can – I will', and then go on to learn, perhaps through failure and defeat, a deeper knowledge of one's own sinful self and of Christ as Saviour.

All Christian discipleship begins in ignorance; but, unless, in our ignorance, we are ready to obey Christ's summons 'Follow me', we shall never find what St Paul calls 'the unsearchable riches of Christ'. Here, as elsewhere, it is a case of 'Never venture, never win!'

Now consider the element of wrong motive. Some Oxford dons once fell to discussing the question, 'What is it takes a man into the Christian ministry?' One of them hazarded the suggestion that it was 'the desire to find a platform on which to strut before the public'.

Whether this is true or not, we need not here discuss. It does not matter a brass farthing whether one of the man's motives is a love of the limelight, provided that he has also the genuine conviction that Jesus Christ is 'the master light of all his spiritual seeing', or, as Peter told him at Caesarea Philippi, 'Thou hast the words of eternal life.' And that he is likely to have had such a

59

conviction is shown by the fact that the man has chosen the Christian ministry, and not, say, the law or the stage or politics. A man may begin with motives that are far from pure, but life and the grace of God may be trusted to drive them out.

So with all of us. If we wait until our motives are quite pure, before becoming Christ's men, we may wait till Doomsday. 'If God were a Kantian,' wrote C. S. Lewis, 'who would not have us till we came from the purest motives, who could be saved?' But if, even with our mixed motives, we venture our allegiance and go on sincerely to try to be true disciples, in the end we shall find in Christ what all the saints have found.

It was a fine saying of George Macdonald, the Scottish poet and novelist, to whom, incidentally, C. S. Lewis owed so much: 'Christ is easy to please but hard to satisfy.' He accepts our miserable best, but upon that he insists on building his own. To the truth of this the lives of Christians down nineteen centuries bear the best witness:

> Finding, following, keeping, struggling,
>   Is He sure to bless?
> Angels, martyrs, saints and prophets
>   Answer, Yes.

15

'If I wash thee not'

(John 13.8 AV)

If, putting the time-machine in reverse, you could somehow escape into the distant past, of what moving and memorable occasion would you like to have been an eye-witness? If that question were put to them, many Christians would, I think, answer: 'I should like to have been present in that Jerusalem upper room on that April evening long ago, as St John describes it in the thirteenth chapter of his Gospel.'

The supper had begun – that supper to which all our Lord's Suppers run back – when, according to St Luke, contention arose among his disciples about who should be the greatest. Think of it – Jesus presently going out to the agony in the garden and, later, to crucifixion, and his disciples are still blinded by visions of thrones and crowns! Silently Jesus rises, puts off his coat, procures a basin, and is on his knees washing his disciples' feet.

We are not told with which of them he began. We only know that when he came to Peter that disciple drew up his feet in horror: 'You, Master, washing my feet?' 'Yes, Peter,' said Christ, 'and one day you will know the reason why.' 'Never!' protested Peter. 'Then, if I do not wash you,' replied Christ, 'you are not in fellowship with me.' Then Peter, half comprehending his Master's meaning, cried out: 'Not my feet only. My hands and head as well. Wash me all over.' He asked too much, not knowing he was already fully cleansed, as Jesus now told him: 'A man who has bathed needs no further cleansing.' But he added that no amount of washing would cleanse one of their number who had become the devil's agent.

The foot-washing over, Jesus took his place again at the head of the table. 'Now do you understand what I have done?' he

61

asked. 'If I, your Master, have washed your feet, you also ought to wash one another's feet, for I have given you an example.'

Then, as the supper proceeded, Jesus became deeply agitated. 'Truly, truly I tell you,' he said, 'One of you is going to betray me.' Horror and perplexity came over them. Then Peter, with a nod to the beloved disciple reclining close to Jesus, said: 'Ask him who it is.' 'It is he,' replied Jesus, 'to whom I give this bread after I have dipped it in the dish.' With that he handed the sop to Judas, purse-bearer to the Twelve. And Judas, having taken it, went out. As the door closed behind him, there came a brief glimpse of the murk outside. 'And it was night,' comments the evangelist. Are there four more dramatic monosyllables in all literature? Judas was going out from 'the light of the world' into outer darkness.

The traitor gone, the spirit of Jesus rose again, and in solemn triumph he cried, 'Now is the Son of man glorified.' So he told them of the coming cross in which God would display his full glory in the Son of man. Then, remembering his quarrelling disciples, he gave them his new commandment. 'You are to love one another,' he said, 'as I have loved you. By this shall all men know that you are my disciples if you have love, one to another.'

He is going home, he tells them, home to his heavenly Father. 'Where I am going,' he says, 'you cannot now follow me, but one day you will.' 'But why not?' protests Peter impulsive as ever, 'I will lay down my life for you.' 'Will you indeed?' replies Jesus sadly, 'Ah Peter, Peter, before cockcrow tomorrow morning you will have denied me three times.'

II

A moving chapter and fit prelude to the great fourteenth chapter of John's Gospel. Yet there is *mystery* in it, and, above all, in that dialogue between Jesus and Peter. What does Jesus mean when he says to Peter, 'If I do not wash you, you are not in fellowship with me'?

Mystified by it, many readers of the Gospel go straight on to Jesus' summons to lowly service: 'For I have given you an example, that you also should do as I have done to you.'

Was the whole episode simply an acted parable whose theme

was the glory of humble service to others? This is part of the truth, but far from the whole. If this were all, that mysterious dialogue between Jesus and Peter is an intrusive irrelevance.

Let us look at it again. Recall, first, that all is being enacted in the shadow of the cross, and that the washer of the disciples' feet is the Lamb of God who is taking away the world's sin. Next, consider the verbs which St John uses to describe our Lord's actions. Jesus 'lays aside' his garments, and, the washing over, 'takes them again'. These are the very verbs which Jesus, as the good shepherd, had used of his death and resurrection in the tenth chapter of John's Gospel. Above all, remember that the motif of the whole story is 'cleansing', and that Jesus said to Peter, 'If I do not wash you, you are not in fellowship with me.' The deeper meaning then is that there is no place in his fellowship for those who have not been cleansed from sin by his atoning death.

Jesus' summons to lowly service is therefore the corollary to the foot-washing. Because they are being cleansed by the sacrifice of Christ the Servant Son of God, they must respond by serving others in lowly love. *Noblesse oblige!*

Of course, when Jesus bids them wash one another's feet, it is the spirit – the moral essence – of his act and example, not the letter, which matters. Not crowns and coronets but towels and basins are the insignia of God's kingdom, and he best honours God's Servant Son who is prepared to stoop and serve.

III

What has the whole story to say to us today? Many people there are like Peter before he grasped the meaning of his master's 'If I wash thee not'. They would like to be Christians but see little significance in that end which crowned Christ's saving work, and of which he cried upon the cross, 'It is finished! The work is done!' They are ready to admire his life and praise his moral teaching as they find it in the Sermon on the Mount. What they cannot credit is that without that 'great cross set up on Calvary' and Christ's Easter victory, they would still be, as Paul said, 'in their sins'. This is the 'scandal' – the stumbling-block – for proud modern man who believes that he can save himself, and will not

63

realize that he cannot cleanse his own evil heart which is at the root of all his trouble.

Yet that 'scandal' – a Christ crucified and raised for the forgiveness of our sins – is the very heart of the Gospel. Without it there is no Good News for guilty man. If Christ does not cleanse us by his 'blood' – his stainless life laid down in death for us – we are unredeemed. But if, by faith, we apprehend that on the cross Christ bore our sins that for us that there might be condemnation no more, then we know that we have been 'bought with a price', we want to cry with Peter, 'Lord, wash me all over!', and, knowing this grace wherein we stand, we rejoice in hope of the glory of God.

16

The Meaning of the Cross

(Good Friday)

As on this day, at the ninth hour, in the year AD 30, Jesus Christ died on a Roman cross outside the northern wall of Jerusalem IIis last utterance, St John tells us, was one brief triumphant word '*Tetelestai!*' which, being translated, means, 'It is finished!', or 'The work is done!' And from that day to this a multitude which no man can number have cried 'Amen' to that last word of his, persuaded that when Christ died the divinest work in all history had been carried to a victorious conclusion.

What then was the 'work' which Christ finished on the cross? For what great purpose did he die?

To ask this question is to pose the problem of the atonement, or at-one-ment, that is, the nature of the reconciliation between holy God and sinful man which Christ effected on the cross.

I

First, let it be said that Christ did not come to preach the atonement but that there might be an atonement to preach. Yet on his way to the cross which crowned his earthly work, he gave his disciples hint after vivid hint at the necessity and purpose of his sacrifice. It was a *cup* of suffering, he said, that his heavenly Father had given him to drink. It was a *baptism* in blood whereby many would be cleansed from the defilement of their sin. It was a *road* marked out for him in scripture (Isa. 53) with death in store for him at the end of his journey. It was a *ransom* which as the Servant Son of God he must pay if 'the many' (which is Hebrew 'for all') were to be delivered from the doom which overhung them. So, by one pregnant metaphor after another, Christ signalled at the meaning of his God-given work before it was done.

65

In the quite literal sense of the word, Christ's crucifixion was not a sacrifice, but a miscarriage of justice brought about by Jew and Roman each acting in his own self-interest. But in the Bible the basic principle of sacrifice is that of a representative offering with which the worshipper can identify himself in his approach to God. Moreover, as John Ruskin finely said, 'the great idea of sacrifice is that you cannot save men from death but by facing it for them, or from sin save but by resisting it'. In this sense Christ's death *was* a sacrifice. It was his willingness to accept what men forced on him and see it as a sacrifice which he could offer to God which transformed an act of human sin into an act of divine redemption. In the cross we find a supreme illustration of Joseph's words to his brothers: 'As for you, you meant evil against me, but God meant it for good, to bring it about that many should be kept alive.'

So, praying for his enemies, 'Father, forgive them, for they know not what they do', Christ died on the cross.

II

When after the first Easter and the Day of Pentecost the early Christians summed up their Good News in a little creed, its first article was, 'Christ died for our sins according to the scriptures' (I Cor. 15.3). They are not named, but chief among them must have been Isa. 53, that chapter in which the prophet describes the suffering Servant of the Lord who 'bore the sin of many and made intercession for the transgressors'.

So, later, in the letters which the apostles wrote to their converts, the cross had a quite central place. Whether it is Peter or Paul or John or the Writer to the Hebrews or the Seer of Patmos, on this they agree, that Christ died to loose us from our sins, bore what we should have borne, did for us what we could never have done for ourselves.

III

All down the centuries since, the best minds in the church have striven to explain to men the meaning of the cross in ways they could understand.

All have agreed that the cross reveals the love of God, so

echoing St Paul who wrote to the Romans, 'God shows his love for us in that while we were yet sinners Christ died for us' (Rom. 5.8 RSV).

This is true, as it finds expression in Isaac Watt's great hymn, 'When I survey the wondrous cross'. Yet it is not the whole truth. Christ died not only to reveal God's love to men but in order to *do* something for them which they could never do for themselves.

So, secondly, most Christian thinkers have agreed that Christ himself 'bore our sins in his own body on the tree' (I Peter 2.24). But how? By so identifying himself with our race that he entered for us into the divine judgment that must ever rest upon the sins of men. The cup which Christ had to drink was 'the cup our sins had mingled', and in the agony of Gethsemane, as in the cry of dereliction from the cross, he is seen drinking that cup to the dregs.

No man may claim to have fathomed completely the whole mystery of the cross, for,

> None of the ransomed ever knew
> How deep were the waters crossed.

Yet, by the judgment of many, none perhaps came nearer it than the saintly John MacLeod Campbell of Rhu in his classic study of the atonement, *The Nature of the Atonement* (1856). Christ, he said, offered on the cross a perfect confession of our sins, a confession which could be described as 'a perfect Amen in humanity to the judgment of God on the sin of man'. To the divine wrath against men's sin, he responded, 'Righteous art thou, O Lord, who judgest so'; and by that perfect response he absorbed it, so making possible our forgiveness by holy God.

(Some have objected to this doctrine that no one can confess sins but the sinner. The objection, which rests on an atomistic idea of human personality – as if we humans were all separate and unconnected pebbles on the shore of time – will not stand. Cannot a loving mother make her child's shame her own? And if the sin of others can be felt, it can also be confessed, not indeed as our own, but as that of those whom we love.)

Here a homely illustration may help to make the doctrine of the atonement clearer.

67

You and I are like the boy who has misbehaved badly and been sent to his room in disgrace. There he sits, sullen and resentful. Suddenly he becomes aware of his elder brother entering the room. 'Surely he hasn't done wrong also!' he muses. Then on his elder brother's face he sees a look he cannot quite fathom. It almost looks as if he were glad to be there. Thereupon the elder brother says to him: 'All is forgiven. Father will take you back, for my sake. Come with me.' So, shamefacedly, the boy goes. But, as he comes into his father's presence, he catches the same look on his face as he had seen on his elder brother's. And the father takes his erring child into his arms and forgives him. ·

Such is Christ's 'work' *for* us. As St Paul said, we are 'accepted in the Beloved'. Yet, to be really effective, it must also become Christ's work *in* us. And this it becomes when we put our whole trust, for this world and the next, in our crucified and living Lord, when round the holy table we partake of Christ's 'love-tokens to his body the church', and when, in our every-day living we seek to serve our fellow men in love, for the sake of him who first loved us, and died and rose again for our salvation.

17

The Unfading Victory

(I Cor. 15.57   Easter Day)

This is 'V-Day' in the church. Today we commemorate the greatest victory in history. The resurrection is the greatest victory of all time because, while the victories of other conquerors – your Alexanders, Caesars and Napoleons – grow old and fade from the memories of men, this victory abides. It abides, because the Victor abides. 'Christ being raised from the dead dies no more. Death has no more dominion over him.'

Rightly do 'we sing the praise of him who died'. On the cross Christ died, by his Father's appointing, to save men from their sins. But the cross is really a terrific question-mark against the sky. If the story of Jesus ends there, we are still, as Paul said, 'in our sins'; there is no good and loving heavenly Father at the heart of things, and we 'are of all men most miserable'. But, thanks be to God, the story does not end there at the cross. The cross does not stand alone. Cross and resurrection are but two parts of one great redeeming act of God, the second of which illumines, as with a shaft of light, the darkness of the first. Easter Day is the interpretation of Good Friday. The resurrection is the making manifest by miracle of the victory of God's saving purpose which took Christ to the cross. It is the Father's seal set upon his Son's sacrifice. We do well to fix our gaze on Calvary; but we never see it aright till we see it with the light of the first Easter morning breaking behind that cross upon the lonely hill.

Lift up your hearts, then, this Easter Day, and think now of the resurrection first as fact, then as experience, and finally as hope.

The resurrection of Christ is, first, *a fact of history*. Once in the annals of mankind one man left a gaping tomb in the wide grave-yard of the world, and this man's victory is like the breaching of a North Sea dyke, an event of apparently small importance whose consequences are incalculable. 'Yes, yes,' you say, 'but how long ago it was! Is the thing really true?'

Well, I give you my opinion, as one who has long studied it, that the evidence is abundant and impressive. The earliest evidence of all – that in the opening verses of I Corinthians 15 – goes back to within five years of the event itself and is part of what has been called 'the oldest Christian document we possess'. It goes back to a time when there were literally hundreds still living who, with their own eyes, had seen the risen Christ, so that Paul can say, in effect, 'If you don't take my word for it, ask them.'

Further, remember that that evidence has been weighed and sifted as no other evidence ever has been. Yet, when all tests have been applied, two things in it stand out unshaken:

1. Joseph of Arimathea's rock tomb had lost its tenant.
2. Christ appeared alive to many people and spoke with them.

Now, it is open to you, if you want to play the sceptic, to try to find other 'explanations' for these facts. Many have tried it, but their explanations have been singularly unconvincing. Even if the sceptic could explain away the empty tomb and Christ's appearances, there would still remain certain other facts which make no sense – unless the Christian claim is true.

One of them is *the silence of the Jews*. For them, Jesus was an impostor who had died the death he deserved. Yet not many days after, this impostor's followers were making Jerusalem ring with the news that he had risen. Clearly if the Jews could have shown this news to be false, they would have done so. But they did not. Why? Because they could not.

Second, there is *the change in the disciples*. Cowards had become heroes, almost overnight. Only the resurrection will explain why men who, at Calvary, 'all forsook him and fled', were ready, a week later, to face any danger for his sake.

Finally, there is *the existence of the church*. For, make no mistake, it was upon the resurrection that the church was built. Let me put it this way. You and I live in a real world in which we can argue back from effects to causes. Thus, when a tidal wave hits the shore, we can guess at the force of the upheaval which caused it. Now the existence of the church rests wholly upon the resurrection. Had there not been men and women who could testify, 'We have seen the Lord', certain it is that the church would never have come into existence. What kind of upheaval produced that tidal wave? Only the fact of the resurrection will explain the existence – and the persistence for 1900 years – of the church. But the fact does not stand alone. There is the experience.

II

By this we mean *men's experience of the living Christ*. When Christ rose from the dead, he did not rise to the old life – he passed into a different mode of being. He passed from this to the spiritual world. But did this mean that he had forsaken his own? On the contrary, he became more real to them than ever. He came back to them as a spiritual presence: he was with them, he lived in them.

You may remember James Denney's famous paradox: 'No disciple ever remembered Christ'? No, they had no need to. He was still with them, unseen but not unknown. He stood by them in their dangers. He was with them when they broke the bread at the Lord's Supper.

This is what is meant by the resurrection as experience. Nor is it only something that the first Christians experienced. It is an experience which may still be ours also:

> Shakespeare is dust and will not come
> To question from his Avon tomb;
> And Socrates and Shelley keep
> An Attic and Italian sleep . . .
> They see not. But, O Christians who
> Throng Holborn and Fifth Avenue,
> May you not meet, in spite of death,
> A Traveller from Nazareth?

Down nineteen centuries Christ's followers have borne the same glad testimony. 'Jesus Christ came to me last night,' says Samuel Rutherford of his Aberdeen gaol, 'and every stone glowed like a ruby.' 'Christ is alive, as alive as I am myself,' cries Dr Dale of Birmingham in his study, as the reality of the risen Lord comes to him like 'a burst of sudden glory'. 'I have had personal dealings with the risen Christ as my Saviour,' testifies P. T. Forsyth, 'nearer and dearer than my own flesh and blood.' 'He comes to us,' wrote Albert Schweitzer, 'as he came to them by the Lakeside; and he speaks to us the same word, Follow me!' It is the testimony of Christ's people still today: like Ray Palmer they can say:

> I see thee not, I hear thee not,
> Yet are thou oft with me,
> And earth hath ne'er so dear a spot
> As where I meet with thee.

III

Finally, the resurrection is a *hope* – our hope. 'Because I live,' said Jesus, 'you shall live also.' Or, as St Paul puts it, the Christian hope is that those who are 'in Christ', that is, in faith-union with him, will one day be 'with Christ' for ever.

The Gospel is not a promise of 'pie in the sky when you die' for all and sundry. It does not proclaim that all go automatically to heaven. But it does proclaim that Christ is a living and universal Lord, that by faith and love we may be made one with him as the twig is grafted into the tree, and that, thus united with him, we too may hope to vanquish 'the last enemy' and share his deathless life.

Therefore in a world where so many things are shaken I invite you to build your faith on the things that cannot be shaken, and especially on the fact of the living Christ. Let no man rob you of your Easter hope. Hold fast to your risen Saviour. Strive to be what every Christian church should be, 'a community of the resurrection'. And take to yourselves the words of the Apostle:

Wherefore, my beloved brethren, be ye steadfast, unmoveable, always abounding in the work of the Lord, forasmuch as ye know that your labour is not in vain in the Lord.

18

The Heavenly Fire

(Luke 12.49)

Do you remember the old Greek fable about Prometheus – the man who stole fire from heaven and brought it to mortal men? Jesus here proclaims himself the new, the true Prometheus, sent by his Father to set the divine fire blazing in the world.

Fire has long been a symbol for the divine presence and power. Think of Moses, in the lone Midian desert, finding God in a bush that burned, or of the pillar of fire that guided wandering Israel in the wilderness. Or think of the prophet Jeremiah describing the Word of God committed to him as 'a burning fire shut up within his bones'. And was not the ever-burning fire on the altar in the Temple at Jerusalem a sign for the Israelites of the continual presence of God?

Turn to the New Testament, and it is a like story. John the Baptist prophesies of God's coming Messiah, or Saviour, 'He shall baptize you with the holy Spirit and with fire.' The Messiah appears, and his message is, 'I am come to send fire on the earth.' And when he has run his course and finished his God-appointed work, seven weeks after the first Easter Day, the Holy Spirit descends at Pentecost upon his followers 'in tongues as of fire'.

If now, leaving the scriptures, we come down the Christian centuries, we find the same tale being repeated. To George Fox, founder of the Quakers, the Lord comes like spiritual flame, and he records in his journal, 'Then did there appear a pure fire within me.' In like manner he comes also to John Wesley on that memorable night in Aldersgate Street, Oxford, and he writes in his diary, 'I felt my heart strangely warmed.'

Most dramatic of all is the experience of Blaise Pascal, the

74

great French scientist and mathematician. He stitches a written record of it into his doublet where, after his death, men find it, and read with wondering eyes, these words:

This year of Grace, 1654, November the twenty-third, from about half past ten to about half past twelve,
Fire!
The God of Abraham, of Isaac, and of Jacob, God not of the philosophers and the scientists, the God of Jesus Christ –
Certitude! Joy!

Thus, down two thousand years, men have experienced the invassion of their lives by God in Christ and called it 'the fire of God'.

II

With all this in mind, let us return to the words of Jesus with which we began – words which reveal the tension in the kindest of all hearts between his own tenderness and the hardness of the task appointed for him by his Father: 'I am come to send fire on the earth, and how I wish it were already kindled! But I have a baptism to undergo, and how straitened I am until it be accomplished!'

Here by 'baptism' Christ means his own *red* baptism, his baptism not in water but in blood. 'My mission,' he is saying, 'is to kindle God's fire in the world. O that it were even now blazing there! But, before this can be, I must go the way of the cross, for only by my sacrificial death can that fire be kindled. That past, I shall be liberated for my wider work, and the heavenly fire will blaze for men's salvation.'

If this is sound interpretation, then on the Day of Pentecost – the day when the Holy Spirit came upon Christ's followers in 'tongues as of fire' – our Lord's great wish came true. 'On that day,' as Bengel, the old German biblical scholar, put it: 'The fire was *lit*.'

III

And from that day to this, through dark ages and bright, the fire Christ kindled has gone on burning, purifying sinners from their

75

sin and transforming them into his own image, the image God would have his children bear.

For the fire of the Gospel, what is it but the burning love of God – his holy passion for man's salvation – shown once for all at Calvary and now, by the Holy Spirit, shed abroad in human hearts today. 'Let us now turn aside,' wrote Dora Greenwell, speaking of the cross, 'and look upon this great sight, of Love that burneth with fire and is not consumed.' And is not the proclamation of the divine love which in Christ suffered unto blood for us men and for our salvation, still today heart-warming news for our sin-sick and fear-ridden world? Still today, whenever and wherever the Gospel is faithfully preached, God comes in it saying to all of us: 'You are sinners and need forgiveness. You are impotent and need power. You are in darkness and need light. Come, then, I offer you the fire of the Gospel. Take it, and it will burn the evil out of you. Take it, and I will light a new lamp of hope in your breast. Take it, and I will make you what I designed you to be – new men and women in Christ, and co-heirs with him of life eternal.'

IV

There is one thing more to say. In the present sad state of the world, with its rampant materialism, its warring ideologies, its 'permissive society' and its sexual libertarianism, all true Christians are praying for a real religious revival. The thing is this: as the Gospel is spiritual fire, so the secret of revival is the burning heart.

'Did not our heart burn within us?' said the two disciples on the Emmaus Road after the risen Christ had made himself known to them in the breaking of the bread. What we need today is people like these – 'incandescent people' – people aflame with the love of the living Lord. Cold hearts will never do it; only warm hearts will; for one burning heart sets another aflame, till the hallowed fire spreads, and, instead of one burning heart, we have a whole fellowship – a church – on fire!

So, as you long for religious revival, be yourself, as St Paul exhorts, 'fervent in spirit', maintain the spiritual glow, and strive, by your own living example, to multiply the number of those aflame with the heavenly fire.

For what makes the heart to burn? There is another saying of our Lord's, not found in our canonical gospels, but preserved for us by the early church father, Origen of Alexandria: 'He that is near me, said Jesus, is near the fire, and he that is far from me is far from the Kingdom.' Here is the secret of the burning heart. Nearness to the living Christ, by the power of the Holy Spirit, nearness to him day by day and not only on Sundays, nearness to him in prayer and sacrament and everyday Christian service to our fellowmen – this is the secret of the heart that burns.

So let the prayer of all of us who profess to be Christians be that of Charles Wesley:

> O Thou who camest from above
>   The pure celestial fire to impart,
> Kindle a flame of sarced love
>   On the mean altar of my heart!

'I am come to send fire on the earth,' said Jesus. Even so, come Lord Jesus, through the Holy Spirit, come to each one of us, and set our hearts aflame!

19

'The Spirit gives life'

(II Cor. 3.6 Whitsunday)

In 1965, not long before he died, the great Swiss theologian, Karl Barth, was asked what he thought of the religious situation in Britain and on the Continent. 'What we are seeing,' he replied, 'is flat-tyre Christianity. The *pneuma*, which is Greek for both "air" and "spirit", has gone out of it, and everybody knows what happens to a pneumatic tyre when it loses its *pneuma*!'

To say that for many Christians today the Holy Spirit is the most unreal part of their faith is to state the obvious. Nor do we help matters by continuing to use the archaic and misleading word 'Ghost'.

How different it was in the springtime of Christianity, as we may read in the Acts of the Apostles! Come to that book with really fresh eyes and you cannot mistake the importance the first Christians attached to the coming of the Holy Spirit as something utterly new. It was like the setting up of a kind of wireless between heaven and earth that was not there before. Because of this 'Anonymous Third Person in their midst', it was possible for every congregation to become a replica of the Galilean circle, with the risen Christ still among them, messages continually coming and going. As for St Paul, you can no more understand his gospel without the Holy Spirit than you can understand our modern civilization without electricity.

All this began to happen on the Day of Pentecost, the first Whitsunday. On that day (we read in the second chapter of Acts) Christ's followers 'were all together in one place', in Jerusalem. Of course they knew that by raising Christ from the dead God had done something unique and marvellous; but, as yet, they did not thrill with 'joy and peace in believing', or feel

78

impelled to carry their good news to a wider world. Yet, that day, seven weeks after the first Easter, something tremendous happened, something which later they could only liken to 'a mighty wind' and 'tongues as of fire'. (One is reminded of the fiery 'photisms' which later Christians like the Frenchman Pascal and the Quaker George Fox were to experience at their conversions.)

If there is one experience hard to put into words, it is man's encounter with the living God. Try to recall the most vivid experience you have ever had of God's presence, then multiply it tenfold, and you may begin to understand what happened on that day of Pentecost. The Spirit of God – and the word 'spirit', in both Hebrew and Greek means 'wind' or 'breath' – came upon these men and so changed them that the bystanders thought them under the influence of a different kind of spirit. 'These men have been drinking!', they said.

What in fact the Holy Spirit was doing was to fuse so many individuals into a fellowship which in the same moment was caught up into the life of their risen Lord. The Spirit gave new life to them, not simply as individuals but as members of a new community, with a mission to the world.

The church of Christ had sprung into dynamic existence, and it was all the doing of the Spirit of God, as prophets like Joel and Ezekiel had predicted centuries before. And it was this same Spirit who was to inspire Christ's apostles, in three short decades, to carry their Good News from Jerusalem to Rome.

II

How stands the case today? Are there not among us many who, depressed by the religious apathy all around them, feel moved to cry with the woman in old Israel when the ark of the Covenant was lost: 'Ichabod! Ichabod! The glory has departed!' Yet the fault is not in our stars but in ourselves. God's gift to the church at Pentecost has not been withdrawn. It is we who have stopped believing in the Holy Spirit, so that the *Geist* (which is German for 'spirit') has gone out of our Christianity.

We are not alone in this. It has happened before, for example, in the rationalistic eighteenth century. Was it not Joseph Butler, the philosopher and Bishop of Bristol, who told John Wesley: 'You pretend to extraordinary manifestations of the Holy Ghost. That is a very horrid thing.' To this the best answer was Wesley's own great ministry which, by the judgment of good historians, saved these islands of ours from the red Revolution which overtook France.

Then suddenly and unpredictably – for the Spirit, like the wind, 'bloweth where it listeth' – men have returned to belief in 'the Lord, the Life-giver', as the Nicene Creed names him, and the church, recovering its lost radiance, begins again to enjoy seasons of refreshment and renewal. Is not this in fact what we are witnessing in some parts of Christendom today?

I am referring, of course, to what is called Neo-Pentecostalism. Starting some fifty years ago among some American negroes, it has spread through the United States and spilled over into Europe and Britain. Today it is the fastest growing movement in Christendom; and where it has gone, it has revitalized moribund churches and promoted warmer Christian fellowship. What is their secret? The Neo-Pentecostals are in no doubt. They claim to have re-discovered the Holy Spirit. How shall we appraise the whole movement?

Here St Paul can help us. Long ago, in Corinth, he had to deal with a Pentecostal Christianity, and in I Cor. 14 we have his considered judgments on it. No Christian had ever a firmer belief in the Holy Spirit; but, by the same token, he was fully alive to the dangers of the Corinthians' Pentecostalism, and especially their evaluation of the Spirit's various gifts. He was himself (he tells us) an expert in 'speaking with tongues', that is, escstatic speech under stress of strong religious emotion requiring an interpreter. But he comes down decisively in favour of spiritual gifts like 'prophecy' (inspired preaching) which edify, or build up, the whole congregation. And in his last sentences he lays it down that 'all things must be done decently and in order', since 'our God is not a God of disorder but of peace'.

Similarly today there are in Neo-Pentecostalism features which are open to criticism – one thinks, above all, of the Neo-Pentecostals' insistence on 'speaking with tongues' as the indispensable mark of possession by the Spirit.

What none can deny is their manifest 'newness of life' and fervour of spirit; and when John Mackay of Princeton, that wise statesman of the ecumenical church, declares, 'If it is a choice between the uncouth life of the Pentecostals and the aesthetic death of the older Western churches, I for one choose life,' many would agree with him.

III

'Not by might, nor by power, but by my Spirit, saith the Lord,' said the prophet long ago (Zech. 4.6). What we in these 'older Western churches' must realize is that the Pentecostal gift is still available for us today.

Somewhere above the low valley along which humanity today is toiling with weary and bleeding feet, the rivers of life which have their source in the Spirit of God are still springing in the sun; and, as we long for a Christian renaissance, it is time to hark back to them for our healing.

Once, long ago, there came by night to Jesus in Jerusalem a teacher in Israel named Nicodemus, curious to know more about the religious revival then sweeping the land. 'What you need,' Jesus told him, 'is such a re-orientation of your whole life as can only be likened to new birth.' 'Impossible!' replied the literal-minded Nicodemus. 'How can a man be born again when he is old?' Then, as the two talked together, the night wind rustled about their place of meeting. 'Listen to the wind, Nicodemus!' said Jesus. 'Whence it comes and whither it goes is a mystery. Yet how real a power it is! So is God's wind, the Spirit. It offers you what you need.'

Are not many of us twentieth-century Nicodemuses? Is there not in our Lord's parable about the night wind a word of God for us today? Too long infected by the humanistic thought of our time, we have been getting along with a Christianity devoid of that spiritual dynamic and enthusiasm which is ever a sign of the presence and power of the Spirit of God.

Doubtless our churches need restructuring in order to meet the new conditions and challenges of the day, as our traditional ways of worship call for refurbishing. But is not our prime need for that change of heart which only 'the Lord, the Life-giver' can create? It is the Spirit who gives life', as the prayer of each one of us should be:

> Breathe on me, Breath of God,
> Fill me with life anew.

20

The Underpinning Ultimates

(II Cor. 13.14   Trinity Sunday)

G. K. Chesterton once observed that, if you ever found yourself renting a room from a landlady, your first question should not be about the food or the furniture she could offer you. No, it would be far better to fix her with a steady eye and ask, 'Madam, what is your total view of the universe?'

Is that really as absurd as it sounds? Isn't the really important thing just what you believe about the ultimate realities which underpin your life?

If you had asked St Paul what were the ultimate realities which underpinned his life, he would have answered, 'Why, the grace of the Lord Jesus Christ, and the love of God, and the fellowship of the Holy Spirit.'

Suppose, on this Trinity Sunday, we spend a little time thinking about them.

I

'The grace of the Lord Jesus Christ.' That is the first one. But what does 'grace' mean?

It is the English equivalent of the Greek word *charis*. To begin with, *charis* meant 'that which gives pleasure'. When the old Greeks used it, they linked the word with loveliness. Then came the Gospel, baptizing the word with new meaning, so that henceforth 'grace' became twin sister to love. So, in the New Testament, 'grace' means wonderful kindness, the kindness that takes your breath away when you realize how little you deserve it. And the grace of Christ? It is simply his wonderful kindness to sinners, that kindness in action. You remember how he came long ago to the woman that was a sinner, to little Zacchaeus of Jericho, to

83

all the last, the least and the lost, to the penitent thief on the cross.

Well, Jesus, after he had risen, made a promise, 'Lo, I am with you always.' And ever since he has been coming to men and women like that, 'unseen but not unknown'. When Samuel Rutherford of Anwoth lay a prisoner for his faith in an Aberdeen gaol, he testified in his diary, 'Jesus Christ came to me in my cell last night, and every stone glowed like a ruby.'

It is the witness of the saints that Christ, the living Christ, still comes to them, so that they can say with Ray Palmer in his hymn:

> I see Thee not, I hear Thee not,
> Yet art thou oft with me.

We all need that grace. We all may have it. This is the first divine reality undergirding our life as Christians.

II

The second is 'the love of God'. The Greek word here is *agapē*. Nowadays, when the word 'love' can mean almost everything from Hollywood to Heaven, it is hardly a satisfactory translation. Neither will 'charity' do, for it is a word which has come down in the world of words. Today men say, 'We don't want your charity'. The best English equivalent for *agapē* is 'caring'. Just try it out: 'God so cared for the world . . .' 'Thou shalt care for thy neighbour as thyself.' Yet, to be frank, it is not the translation but the *truth* of the phrase which perplexes many today. They look out on the world with all its chaos and its cruelty, and they say, 'Does God really care?'

Well, the world contains comparatively few out-and-out atheists – people who have really thought things through and decided that there is no God. Common sense tells most men that the world must have been called into existence by some kind of great power or another. The question is, What kind of power? Is it good? Is it bad? Or is it just indifferent?

Now, like St Paul, we Christians believe that it is good, we believe that the power which 'moves the sun and the other stars'

84

is not a thing but a person, not a fate but a Father, and a Father who cares.

Why do we believe this? We believe it because of the fact of Christ. Like the men of the New Testament we find our clue to the riddle of the world in him. We believe that the Supreme Being we call God not only called this world into existence and still keeps his controlling hand on it, as in history he is

> sifting out the hearts of men
> Before his judgement seat,

but that once he came right down into it as a man, to show us what he is like, and then, by the cross of Calvary, to tell us how much he cared. So, when we are asked, 'How can you be sure of the love of God?', we point to 'that strange man upon his cross'. 'He who has seen me,' said Christ, 'has seen the Father.' We see the Saviour on his cross, and we say, 'God loves – like that!' Or we see Christ risen from the dead in all his Easter glory, and we cry, 'Behold the omnipotent love of the Father!'

'God, Thou art love! I build my faith on that,' said the poet; and so say we. 'The love of God' – why, It is the only thing that puts a meaning into this strange, riddling, bitter-sweet thing we call 'life'. The love – the caringness – of God, shown in the blood of Calvary and in the shining miracle of the resurrection – this is the second spiritual fact underpinning our lives as Christians.

III

And now this other one – the fellowship (or companionship) of the Holy Spirit.

If you find the Christian doctrine of the Holy Spirit hard to understand, as many do, remember that it means quite simply 'God here – here and now – and not simply in the Holy Land nineteen centuries ago.' It is, as Henry Scougal put it, 'the life of God in the soul of man', your soul and mine, now.

The Holy Spirit is the invisible power of God which, descending on God's people on the Day of Pentecost, has been working in them ever since. He is Christ's *alter ego*, or other self, sent not so much to supply his absence as to accomplish his presence, and

85

serve us as interpreter, comforter (i.e., strengthener) and helper as we walk the Christian way.

It is the Holy Spirit who illumines for us the words of scripture and turns them into the Word of God.

It is the Holy Spirit who helps us when, in times of trouble or of decision, we seek divine guidance in prayer (Rom. 8.26).

It is the Holy Spirit who, in times of bereavement, enables Christian men and women to bear their bitter loss.

It is the Holy Spirit who enables us to confess Jesus Christ as our Saviour and Lord (I Cor. 12.3).

In short, the Holy Spirit is the divine power which inspires all true and lovely and heroic Christian living:

> And every virtue we possess,
> And every victory won,
> And every thought of holiness
> Are His alone.

Shall we sum up? What are the three divine realities under-pinning the Christian's life? The answer is: the wonderful kindness of Christ, the Son, the infinite care of God the Father, and the strong help of the Holy Spirit. Did I say three? Then I am wrong. For the three are one – the Holy Trinity, Father, Son and Holy Spirit, one God, the Triune, blessed for ever.

For almost twenty centuries millions upon millions of men and women have walked through this house of their pilgrimage and gone down at last to the dark river, supported by faith in this triune God.

Will you? Then go forth in that faith, and amid all life's ills and accidents, say with that gallant soldier of the cross, St Patrick:

> I bind unto myself today
> The strong name of the Trinity.

And may the wonderful kindness of Christ the Son, and the infinite care of God the Father, and the strong help of the Holy Spirit be with you, 'right on to the end of the road'.

21

'God's way of righting wrong'

(Rom. 1.17 NEB)

Not a very exciting text, is it? Not the kind to stab a congregation broad awake and make them sit up and take notice! All this talk of Paul's about 'the unrighteousness of men' and 'the wrath of God' – does it not sound like something which may have meant much to folk nineteen hundred years ago, but has precious little bearing on our world and our problems today?

Lots of people think this way about St Paul – if they ever think about him at all. He is just an old fuddy-duddy out of the Bible, no doubt an excellent man in his day, but hardly the man with answers to the questions which now vex us. And yet they are wrong. Pierce below the old-fashioned crust of his words, and you will find that Paul has a word – in fact, the Word – that mankind needs to hear today.

I

First, then, Paul says: 'I am not ashamed of the Gospel.' Now why on earth should Paul – Paul who gloried in the Gospel – talk this way? Why should there be any suggestion of Paul's being 'ashamed of the Gospel'?

The answer lies in one word: Rome. It was the thought of Rome and the prospect of preaching the Gospel there which moved Paul to write the word 'ashamed'. Rome! What glamour there was in the very name! Rome, with all her pomp and power! Rome, where the great Caesar himself dwelt! Rome, the tallest town men had ever built, the metropolis of the mightiest empire the world had ever seen! Make no mistake about it. If you and I had been living in Paul's day, we would have felt the glamour too. Paul felt it. He was proud to call himself a *civis Romanus* – a Roman citizen. And ever since he had become Christ's apostle, he had been nursing a dream, the dream of one day preaching the Gospel in Rome.

Now at last his dream looks like coming true. Soon, God willing, he will visit Rome. Meantime, in Corinth, he writes a letter to the Christians in Rome, to pave the way for his visit. Swiftly in his mind he begins to compare the two things – Rome and the Gospel. How, he wonders, will his Gospel sound in the world's capital? How will he convince those hard-bitten citizens of Rome that in the person of Jesus of Nazareth, crucified some years before in an obscure corner of their vast empire, the great God himself has indeed acted, once and for all, 'for us men and for our salvation'? Will not the lordly men of Rome greet his message with derision and contempt? Just for a moment Paul's confidence wavers. Then he pulls himself together: 'I am not ashamed of the Gospel,' he says, 'for . . .'

Well, we will come to his reason in a moment. Meantime, let us note that this same feeling sometimes comes over us today. We visit one of our great cities – let London or Paris or New York stand for Paul's Rome. There, as in Rome, are all the material evidences of man's skill and ingenuity: his modern 'towers of Babel' – those human filing-cabinets flaunting themselves against the sky – the roar of the internal combustion engine or the thunder of the jumbo jet, all the multitudinous din and power of a great modern city . . .

Perhaps we stop and listen to the people as they pass on their various bits of business. But, as we listen, does the talk ever turn to Jesus and the Gospel? What has 'the old, old story' to do with this modern Vanity Fair? Has it any relevance for this atomic age? For a moment we feel exactly as Paul did. We feel the apparent weakness of the Gospel.

How then did Paul conquer this sense of shame when he thought of the Gospel against the background of imperial Rome? The answer is: he forgot the glamour and got down to hard fact. He remembered that there was *another* side to the medal of Rome's magnificence. And when he reflected on that other side, all Rome's splendour vanished like a burst bubble. For now he remembered that this much-vaunted Roman civilization was rotten – rotten to the very core.

11

'I am not ashamed of the Gospel,' he wrote, 'for (and here is his reason) the wrath of God is revealed from heaven against all ungodliness and wickedness of men.'

'The wickedness of men . . .' Rome was full of it. 'Into Rome,' wrote their own historian Tacitus, 'every foul and horrible thing finds it way sooner or later.' For all her might and magnificence Rome teemed with iniquity. She might bestride the world like a Colossus; she might spread her conquests from the Euphrates to the Thames; but she could do nothing to cleanse and regenerate the victims of lust and sin with which her realms were filled. All Rome's pomp and splendour lay under the divine decree that sin brings death – must end in ruin – unless God could somehow provide a cure. If Paul knew that God had such a cure, might he not well say, 'I am not ashamed of the Gospel'?

Again, let us leave Paul for a moment, and look at ourselves. Are we not much in the same case today? What a clever creature is modern man! What masteries over the material world he can claim! Can he not domesticate the lightning from heaven for use in his kitchen stove, and capture the wandering voices of the ether in a tiny transistor, and split the atom to release illimitable sources of energy, and plant his gleaming space-ships in the immensities of God's universe?

Ah, but this is only one side of the medal, and the other side will hardly bear inspecting. The truth is that modern man, for all his cleverness, is a tragic figure. He prostitutes his great gifts for the manufacture of napalm and atomic bombs – and the result is Hiroshima, Nagasaki, Vietnam and the mass-murder of innocent women and children. He befuddles himself with drink and drugs and under their influence commits crimes of which 'the lower creation' would be ashamed. His great cities abound with gangsters and thugs, and vice, immorality, and race-violence are the order of the day. But need I continue the sorry catalogue? Many things modern man can do; one thing he cannot do – he cannot save himself, cannot cleanse his own evil

89

heart, cannot even live at peace with his fellow-men. These are sombre facts; but who among us, looking out on the world today, would deny their truth?

III

Is there then no hope for him? God forbid! For it is just here that the Gospel comes in. What does Paul say? 'For therein' (i.e., in the Gospel) 'the righteousness of God is revealed.' In the Gospel we have 'God's way of righting wrong', his remedy for our unrighteousness, his cure for our disease. In the Gospel is the one convincing proof that God has not left man to 'stew in his own juice' (as the saying goes) but is resolved upon his rescue. Here is the assurance that for his sins there is forgiveness, for his weakness power, and for his troubled heart, peace.

So never say that what Paul wrote in Romans nineteen hundred years ago has nothing to say to us today. Despite all his material triumphs, man is still the same sin-sick person that Paul knew. And all our man-made remedies – our higher education, our economic planning, our conferences of international statesmen – seem powerless to provide the needed cure. For why? Because,

> The heart aye's the part aye
> That makes us right or wrang.

What mankind needs today is a complete change of heart – such a spiritual renewal as only the Gospel – God's dynamic for saving men, as Paul called it – can produce. Some day, sooner or later, we shall have to realize that the root evil of humanity goes deeper than economic maladjustment, is in fact what the Bible calls 'sin' – the pride and greed of man – and that, if you can cure that, you may hope for a solution to the other problems. Then, perhaps in despair – ever the best soil for it – men will come back to God's remedy for it which we call the Gospel, and casting themselves on the mercy of God, will find there that pardon for their sin, that pattern for a better life, and that power to achieve it, which alone give meaning, purpose and hope to this present life, and also hold out sure promise of a better life to come.

May the good Lord speed that day!

90

22

The Logic of Redemption

(Rom. 8.32)

One of my boyhood's memories in my native Ayrshire is of two middle-aged men – one my own father – warmly disputing which was the finest song Burns ever wrote. Was it 'My love is like a red, red rose', or 'Ae fond kiss, and then we sever', or, perhaps, 'Auld Lang Syne', that song which has gone round the world?

Just so, some of us who regard St Paul as the supreme expert on the Christian faith – its first and greatest interpreter – sometimes debate which was the finest chapter he ever wrote. Some choose Paul's 'Song of Songs' about Christian love in I Cor. 13, others his 'great and comfortable words' about the resurrection in the fifteenth chapter of the same letter. But many – and I am one of them – choose the eighth chapter of his letter to the Romans, maintaining that Paul never spoke with greater inspiration than in the chapter which begins, as a wise old Scots woman put it, 'with no condemnation' and ends with 'no separation'.

From this chapter comes our text: 'He that spared not his own Son but delivered him up for us all, how shall he not with him (Christ) also freely give us all things?'

Teachers of logic speak about 'premisses' and 'conclusions'. A 'premiss' is a proposition stated, or assumed, as a basis for after-reasoning. And what our text gives us in one sentence is what may be called 'the logic of redemption' – its divine premiss and the salutary conclusion which follows from it.

I

'He that spared not his own Son but delivered him up for us all' – this is Paul's premiss. And the first point he would have us grasp is that *everything in the Gospel goes back to the self-sacrifice of God.*

Some people will tell you that the message of the Gospel is, 'God is love'. They would do better to say: 'God so loved the world that he gave his only Son.' For the heart of the Gospel is not an idea but an *act* – an act of God himself in the very stuff of our human history: God's giving of his Son. 'He that spared not his own Son but delivered him up for us all', is how Paul puts it; and at once we are reminded that when Christ died at Calvary, God was there too.

Some of you may have read Richard Jefferies' book *Bevis. The Story of a Boy.* The boy Bevis had a Bible with pictures in it, one depicting the crucifixion. That picture hurt his feelings very much, the cruel nails, the unfeeling spear . . . Long he looked at it, then he turned the page saying, 'If God had been there, he wouldn't have let them do it.'

'If God had been there . . .' There is dramatic irony for you! For the whole Christian religion rests upon the conviction that God *was* there – that Calvary shows us how much it cost God to rescue a world of sinners.

In the cross, seen, as we ever ought to see it, in the light of the first Easter Day, God is saying to us: 'I am no mere spectator of the sins and miseries of men. For their sakes I spared not my own Son. We carried the load of sin and guilt which crushes you. It bowed him into the ground. But, on the third day, by my power, he rose again, with the promise in his hand of a new humanity and a "living hope" of victory over man's last enemy, death.'

Everything therefore in the Gospel of our redemption goes back to God's act of self-sacrifice when he 'spared not his own Son', for us men and for our salvation. This is the first and palmary point – what we have called 'the premiss' – in the logic of redemption.

II

Turn now to the conclusion which Paul draws from it: 'How shall he not with him (that is, Christ), also freely give us all things.'

Commenting on these words James Denney wrote: 'The

Christian faith in Providence is an inference from Redemption. The same God who did not spare his only Son will also freely give us all things.'

So the second great thought of our text is this: *It is because of the cross that we are to be sure of the daily providence of God.* Because He has done the first and greater thing – given his only Son for our saving – we may be sure that he will do the second and lesser thing – guide us and give us all we need.

But 'providence'! What a cold and bloodless word it really is! You never find Christ himself employing abstract terms like 'providence'. He does not say with the old Scottish proverb:

> Confide ye aye in Providence,
> For Providence is kind.

Listen to him talking on the subject in his Sermon on the Mount:

.Your heavenly Father knows that you need all these things. God feeds the wild birds. Will he not much more provide for you? If you, bad as you are, know how to give good gifts to your children, how much more will your heavenly Father give good things to those who ask him.

Here is the doctrine of providence as a child can grasp it. It is the assurance that in all the chances and changes of life there is a great loving Someone Above looking after us whom we can address as 'Father'.

It is *not*, observe, the assurance that God will pamper and spoil us by sparing us all trials and sorrows. So to conceive of God would be to make him like the too indulgent father of many a modern household. Moreover, we must never forget that God ordained a gibbet, and not a bed of roses, for his own well-beloved Son. Accordingly, Christians at least have never held that it was the purpose of God that a good time should be had by all, here and now. How could they when the chief symbol of their religion was a cross? No, trials and tribulations, these things God will use to train and discipline his children in this house of their pilgrimage. But it *is* the assurance that, come weal or woe,

93

God will be with those who trust him and will make all things work together for their good (Rom. 8.28).

Now, if this is what providence means, we may come back to our text. Paul says we can be sure of all this because, in Christ, we know what the great Someone Above is like. He is the One who was willing to give up his only Son for our salvation. The love which did not keep back Christ is watching over your concerns and mine.

'He will also freely give us all things,' Paul says. What are 'all things'? The answer in Christ's own words is '*good* things'. Not fame, or wealth, or unclouded happiness. Such things Christ never promises. 'In the world,' he says, 'you will have trouble' (John 16.33). No, but daily light and leading, daily forgiveness and help, power to keep us sane and strong amid the crises and storms of life, and, at the last, if we are faithful unto death, victory over 'the last enemy', a 'crown of life', and a place in his Father's house on high with its 'many rooms' (John 14.2).

Men and women, do you believe this? And in that faith will you front the world, and the future, and life, and death?

23

Signs, Wisdom and a Cross

(I Cor. 1.22–24)

Some of us have our own ideas of how God ought to do his job; and if he does not do it, we feel free to reject him, like the small boy who said, 'I will pray all week for an engine, and if God doesn't give it to me, I will go and worship idols.'

So St Paul found nineteen hundred years ago. 'Give us miracles,' said the Jews to God. The Greeks of the day said, 'Give us wisdom,' that is, an intellectual key to the world's mystery. But what God gave them was a man on a gibbet. And they didn't like it.

Is it so very different today?

I

'The Jews ask for signs,' Paul writes. It was true. All through Christ's ministry this is what they were asking of him. What they craved was some marvellous act which would blazon the truth of his claims against the sky. If they were to believe in him, they wanted his God to do something 'byordinar' (as the Scots say). But the sign they got was the sign of the cross; and that was anathema to them.

Still today the Jew in many of us asks for such signs. When, for example, the poet Charles Murray declared that, if he were God, and saw what a hell men had made of his 'braw birlin earth', he would 'droon oot the hale hypothec, dicht the sklate', was he not, Jew-like, telling God how he ought to act? It is the state of mind that wants God to interpose spectacularly in human affairs and arrest evil by the fiat of omnipotence.

But God apparently does not do so; and so our modern Jews find here a grave objection to acceptance of the Gospel.

Next, writes Paul, 'the Greeks seek wisdom' – a key to the world's mystery which will approve itself to their human reason and 'justify the ways of God to men'. They bring the Gospel to the test of their reason and judge it 'foolishness'. They cannot demean their proud intellects to believe that God became man in Christ, that Christ died on the cross for their sins, that God raised him from the dead and gave him glory, so that our faith and hope might be in him. So, renouncing the Christian faith, they call themselves 'agnostics' or 'humanists', and retire into the bolt-holes of their own specialisms, putting ultimate questions out of their minds – like the American intellectual who wrote:

> My code of life and conduct is this: work hard, play to the allowable limit, never do a friend a dirty trick, trust to tobacco for calm and serenity, and never allow oneself a passing thought of death.

II

Are then the Jews and the Greeks both wrong in the demands they make? Has the Christian religion nothing to do with power or with wisdom? On the contrary, in a sense they are fair and just demands, demands which any true religion must meet. And meet them, Paul says, God does in Christ and his cross. There, in the cross, you see both the power and the wisdom of God.

Ah, but for our modern Greeks just there is the rub. They cannot, they will not, find their key to the world's riddle in a man who was hanged. Was Paul talking the most arrant nonsense – or, conceivably, the highest and holiest sense?

Let us consider more closely what Paul is saying.

(a) First, the Jew in many of us cries out for evidences of power in God. Where shall we find it? In the tempest, perhaps? Or in the thunderbolt? But is not this how little children and primitive peoples conceive of divine power? Those who know something of the laws of nature know that the fiercest tempest is as nothing compared with the irresistible force of the tide – that no thunderbolt has in it power to match the sunshine of a summer morning. But they know also that God has much harder things to do than can be done by tempest or by lightning. God has to make bad men good. He has to subdue them to penitence and faith. And he has to do this not for one only but for all. He has to reconcile a rebellious world to himself. Precisely, says St Paul, and this is what he is doing through his Son upon his cross. God was in Christ, God is in Christ, reconciling the world to himself.

When Paul was writing, the Gospel had been at work in the world for five and twenty years. Yet even in that short time it had proved itself 'the power of God unto salvation, to the Jew first and also to the Greek', to thousands upon thousands who had put their faith in Christ as the Son of God.

We who live nineteen hundred years later, and are members of a church which now numbers more than a thousand millions on the earth, are in a better position to judge the truth of his words. Look back then down the centuries and tell me what person or event is to be compared with the cross of Christ as a regenerating and reconciling power. Let our modern men make of it what they will, it is ungainsayable fact that for millions upon millions he has proved himself the one great, historic fountain of forgiveness and new life. Even today, in this tragic twentieth century, is there any other real hope for the man who longs to be done with his old life and be reconciled to God? Will all the scientists in the world will all the psychologists – undertake to work this spiritual miracle for him? Only the power of God can do it – that power to save shown at the cross and still, by the testimony of innumerable saved men and women, still operating through it. This is the answer to all who ask for signs – for evidences of power in God.

> I asked them whence their victory came.
> They, with united breath,
> Ascribed their conquest to the Lamb,
> Their triumph to his death.

(b) But, second, 'the Greeks seek for wisdom'; and Paul says that the crucified and risen Christ is God's answer – his answer to their quest for a key to the world's mystery. And is not the apostle right? Is not the mystery of the world – the really baffling one – what Paul calls 'the mystery of iniquity'? And may I suggest that neither our scientists nor our philosophers, for all their cleverness and subtlety, have explained it?

97

Many times they have tried. They have dismissed sin – moral evil – as an unreality, a mere negation. They have pronounced it a 'hangover' from our animal ancestry. They have explained it as 'good in the making'! How 'phoney' these explanations sound today! By the two colossal human disasters of our time, and their awful aftermaths, we have learned in blood and tears how dread a laboratory of good and evil is the heart of man. Belsen and Hiroshima, gas ovens and hydrogen bombs, good in the making! The terrible logic of history has exploded our sky-blue notions of man's natural goodness, unsealing our eyes afresh to 'the mystery of iniquity'.

Now what Paul says is that the only thing which goes any way to make this 'mystery' intelligible is not some human wisdom but the new revelation of divine reality given in the cross. For at the cross, with the eye of faith, we Christians see God in Christ entering into our human situation and, by taking the burden of our sin upon himself, enabling us to find forgiveness and new life:

> O love of God, o sin of man,
> In this dread act thy strength is tried,
> And victory remains with love,
> Jesus our Lord is crucified.

Here is 'wisdom' for a world baffled by sin; here in the cross sin at last gets a meaning as a foil to divine grace; here we see God in Christ redeeming sinful men by loving them to the uttermost.

Do you remember how Robert Browning's Arab physician Karshish put the issue to his friend Abib:

> The very God! Think, Abib; dost thou think?
> So the All-Great were the All-loving too;
> So, through the thunder, comes a human voice
> Saying, 'O heart I made, a heart beats here!
> Face, my hands fashioned, see it in Myself.
> Thou hast no power, nor mayst conceive of Mine;
> But love I gave thee, with Myself to love,
> And thou must love Me, who have died for thee.'

III

Men and women, I cannot prove to you, beyond all your doubting, that this strange man upon his cross is your 'window into God at work', the revelation of the power and wisdom of God. It is still open to you to play the modern Greek and call it 'foolishness'. But I can point you to millions upon millions of people who have found in 'the word of the cross' the highest wisdom given them under this visiting moon, and invite you to make the grand venture of Christian faith.

Make 'the acknowledgment of God in Christ', take Christ to be the revelation of 'the Love that moves the sun and the other stars'; and he will give you things to learn in his school, skills to use in his service, and people to meet and care about for his sake. And to those of you who accept him as Saviour and Lord, as Albert Schweitzer said, 'he will reveal himself in the trials and triumphs you will pass through in his fellowship'; you will learn, as an ineffable mystery, who he is; and peradventure he will become to you, as to Paul – and how many others down the centuries – the very power and wisdom of God.

24

Christianity — Dope or Dynamic?

(I Cor. 3.21–23)

'All things are yours . . . and you are Christ's . . . and Christ is God's.'

What is the Gospel? Dope or dynamic? Ask a communist, and if he knows his Marxist Bible, he will answer: 'It is the opiate of the people' – a form of escapism, 'pie in the sky when you die', in short, a creed which teaches men to fix their starry eyes on another world, when they ought to be rolling up their sleeves to tackle the problems of this one.

Ask St Paul, and he answers: 'The Gospel is the saving power of God for everyone who has faith' (Rom 1.16 NEB), that is, a divine dynamic for saving sinful men.

Well, dope or dynamic – spiritual sedative or spiritual power – which is it?

Let us start by making two admissions. To begin with, let us admit that, if the Gospel is only an opiate or an escape, few people would want to be called Christians. For if men are unhappy, they want more than dope; and if they are happy, they don't want an escape. But is this really the choice which the Gospel offers? We may gravely doubt it.

Again, let us concede that some of us Christians do often give the impression that Christianity, so far from being what Christ claimed to bring, 'a more abundant life', is really a null and negative thing. Where Christ said 'Do', they keep on saying 'Don't' – 'Touch not, taste not, handle not', like the heretics in Colossae long ago (Col. 2.21). Now, if the Gospel is just a dreary catalogue of 'Don'ts', if it consists mostly in slamming the door on the world around us, it isn't much use to us. Most of us are not cut out to be monks in a cloister or nuns in a convent. But is this

100

really what Christianity is all about? When you are faced with a question like this, it is a wise rule to consult an expert on the subject. Now, by common consent Paul was such an expert on Christianity, perhaps the greatest that ever lived. He taught it, he lived it, and he died for it. Let us ask the apostle.

I

This brings us to the first bit of the text: 'All things are yours,' he tells his Christian converts in Corinth, as though they were spiritual multimillionaires. No hint of narrowness, no suggestion of escapism here: 'All things are yours; whether Paul or Apollos or Cephas, or the world, or life or death, or things present or things to come, all are yours.' There's Christian breadth for you! Everything, Paul says, in the world or out of it, everything pleasant or unpleasant, is part of the Christian's programme. In other words, real Christianity is a way to meet and to master all that life holds.

Now is this just pious blah on Paul's lips? Quite the contrary. Study Paul's own life as a Christian, and you will see that it took in everything. His Christianity was not just for the sunny day or for the select few. It was for every day, as it was for all men. And not only did this heroic little man take the then known world for his parish, but he ran the whole gamut of human joy and sorrow under the inspiration of his Christian faith. For him, Christianity was not dope, it was a dynamic – a faith to cover and conquer every circumstance of life.

II

But perhaps you think Paul is just a 'one-off' example out of the long ago. Very well, then, take a twentieth-century example. Many of you must have heard of Dr Edward Wilson, chief scientific officer to Captain Scott's ill-fated expedition to the South Pole. (Some of you may even have read George Seaver's splendid *Life* of him.) Edward Wilson was a true modern saint. 'So long as I have stuck to Nature and the New Testament,' he declared, 'I have only got happier every day.' He was utterly unselfish, and in times of stress his colleagues leaned on him as on a rock. Every danger in what came to be called 'the worst journey in the world' he met with indomitable courage. His friends agreed that his was the most Christ-like life they had ever known. Yet he seldom talked religion, and only when his diaries were later discovered, did the secret of his life come out, his deep and steadfast Christian faith, the faith which made him write from the tent of death to his wife: 'Don't be unhappy. All is for the best. We are playing a good part in a great scheme arranged by God himself. And all is well.'

Not much escapism about that life. To Edward Wilson his Christian faith was not a drug but a dynamic, even in the dark valley of death.

And wherever you get the real thing, it is the same story. True Christianity does not turn its back on the world and retreat into some cosy cloister. It faces it, clear-eyed and unafraid. It is a way to meet and master all that life holds, now as much as in Paul's day. But how? What is the secret?

III

For an answer, turn to the second piece of the text. All things are yours,' Paul writes, 'and you are Christ's.' 'You belong to Christ.' Somehow the secret is bound up with belonging to Christ. Well, doubtless you have heard that kind of thing before. It sounds like a pious platitude, a typical evangelical *cliché*. But is it? What does it mean? Why, it means that the essential thing in Christianity is *a personal relationship to Christ*.

Now it is just here that many of Christianity's critics get it wrong. They say, 'I'm not a professing Christian, because I can't accept the church's attitude to this or that question' – let us say, 'pools', or pacifism, or abortion. They assume that Christianity is just a set of opinions about this or that question of the day. So they brew up their own idea of Christianity – and then say that they don't like it.

We don't like it either, their idea of Christianity. For, though being a Christian means taking up quite definite attitudes to evil, whether in public or in private life, the heart of it is not a set of opinions at all, but a personal relationship to a person, a living person, the risen and reigning Christ who is head of the body which is the church.

102

'You are Christ's,' says the apostle. This suggests the Christian's standard of judgment in all things. Christ is the pattern of his thinking and doing. Christ is his Lord and Master to whom he rejoices daily to commit himself anew in trust and obedience. Not opinions about this or that question of the day, but a personal relationship to a living Lord – this is the essential, the basic thing, in Christianity.

IV

So to the last bit of the text: 'And Christ is God's.' Here we may imagine some free-thinker, agnostic, or humanist saying: 'If you Christians choose to make Christ your private hero, that is your own concern. Now, if this Christ of yours were something more than this, if somehow he were bound up with the ultimate meaning of things, it would be quite a different matter.'

But this is precisely what Paul now asserts: 'And Christ is God's.' So far from being merely some people's private hero, he is part of the last reality in the universe. He is God's. When Paul says 'God', he means the power that holds the wheeling planets in their courses and directs the course of history. So far from Christ being just a piece of our human experience, the supreme truth about the Carpenter of Nazareth is that he comes from the Creator. And when we build on Christ, as we Christians do, we are building not on shifting quicksands but on the eternal granite which is God. Nay more, as Principal Cairns said memorably during the last World War, 'when your feet are on that rock, you can exult even in the whirlpool'.

Thus in Paul's three staccato sentences we get three clues to what Christianity really is.

First, so far from being an escape from life, it is *the* way of life – the way to meet and, with God's help, master every crisis that life may hold for you.

Second, the secret of this way of life is a personal relationship to a living person, Christ.

And, last, in building upon Christ, we are building upon bedrock, on ultimate reality, on God – that God who so loved this fallen world of ours that he gave his own Son for its saving.

25

Koinōnia

(I John 1.3)

Sir Edwyn Hoskyns, the great Cambridge theologian, used to speak of burying oneself in a lexicon and rising in the presence of God. He meant that there were words in the New Testament which, when you study them, like an 'Open Sesame', admit to divine secrets. Wrestle with their meaning, and they will lead you, as with an Ariadne's thread, to the heart of the Christian faith.

Take, for example, that little four-lettered word *Abba*, meaning 'dear Father'. It is the word Jewish children used at home when addressing their earthly fathers – an every-day, family word. Yet precisely in this fact lay its offence for many of our Lord's contemporaries. No pious Jew would have dreamt of addressing the Almighty with this homely word. The fact that Jesus – *and he alone* – did just this, is remarkable testimony to the kind of communion he had with God, to that sense of unshared Sonhood with a heavenly Father which was his.

All this may serve as introduction to another important New Testament word. It is the Greek word *koinōnia*, whose root meaning is 'sharing'. In our English translations of the New Testament it is sometimes rendered 'communion', and sometimes 'fellowship'. We still talk today, as St Paul did to the Galatians, of 'the right hand of fellowship', as we still call the Lord's Supper 'Communion.' More, does not our weekly worship commonly conclude with the prayer that 'the fellowship of the Holy Spirit', i.e., the fellowship which the Spirit creates – may be with us all.'

In the New Testament this word *koinōnia* has two orientations – a vertical and a horizontal – as behind this Greek word lies the whole story of Christ and his disciples as well as the experience of the early church.

104

I

All began in Galilee when Jesus appointed twelve men that 'they might be with him' and become the nucleus of the new Israel he was called of God to create. 'You have not chosen me,' he said, 'but I have chosen you.' It was he who initiated the fellowship – the fellowship that was to grow ultimately into what today we call the church catholic, or universal.

We need not here repeat the story of his earthly ministry – how in the months, the years that followed, the fellowship was tested, tried and tempered, through many sweet and bitter days. Let us pass to an April evening on the day before the Jewish Passover in the year AD 30. The scene is an upper room in Jerusalem, and, to all appearances, that fellowship between Jesus and his twelve men is coming to an abrupt and irrevocable close. Yet, though a cross awaits him on the morrow, Jesus, the host at the Last Supper, does not think so. Solemnly, deliberately, he makes provision for their future fellowship beyond the cross. The simplest every-day things – bread and wine – he makes the pledges – the love-tokens – of a fellowship that will continue by and through his atoning death. After his resurrection the fellowship will go on, will grow, will expand from small beginnings to great endings.

And it does. Open the book of Acts at chapter 2: 'And they continued steadfastly in the *koinōnia*,' we read. Though the risen Lord is now at the right hand of his Father, they are not conscious of being 'orphans'. 'No apostle,' wrote James Denney in a famous paradox, 'ever remembered Christ.' They had no need to. Had he not promised, 'Lo, I am with you always', and had he not kept his promise?

Through the Holy Spirit's power, he is still with them, leading, guiding, and inspiring them. They begin to realize that their fellowship is not meant for themselves alone but for all men, that it is a fellowship not 'thirled' to the dear, dead days in Galilee, but belonging to the timeless and eternal. It is a fellowship that even death cannot sever; and when they 'fall asleep' (to use the New Testament's metaphor for dying), they are convinced that, having been '*in* Christ', they are but going to be '*with* Christ' in his Father's house on high.

105

Nor is theirs only a continuing fellowship; it is also a *transforming* one. Gradually they find by experience that as they keep *koinōnia*, they are becoming different men – are being shaped, by God's Spirit, to the likeness of his Son – so that even their foes are constrained to take note that 'these men have been with Jesus' and to exclaim, 'See how these Christians love one another!' And when they are asked the secret of this moral miracle, they reply, as St John did: 'Our fellowship is with the Father and with his Son Jesus Christ.'

This, then is Christian *koinōnia*, then and now, on its vertical side – a partnership with the heavenly Father and his crucified and living Son, Jesus Christ.

II

But the *koinōnia* of which we speak has also a horizontal side to it. 'We have fellowship one with another,' says St John.

Right from the beginning the first Christians realized this. 'All that believed,' we read in Acts, 'were together.' This Christian 'togetherness' the apostles keep stressing again and again in their letters. Have you noticed, for example, how Paul sprinkles his pages with compounds of the Greek preposition *sun*, which means 'together with'? *Sunergoi, sundouloi, sunstratiōtai, sunklēronomoi* – that is, 'fellow-workers, fellow-servants, fellow-soldiers, fellow-heirs' – is how he describes his friends and helpers. Call this camaraderie, if you will; but it is a holy camaraderie, a camaraderie 'in Christ' – a fellowship which continues Christ's work in the world, that serves and suffers as he did, a fellowship in all the burdens and blessings of the Gospel.

III

But the range and compass of the fellowship goes still further. 'Our capital city,' Paul tells the Philippians, 'is in heaven.' Or, as Moffatt translates it, 'We are a colony of heaven.' Says the Writer to the Hebrews, 'We are compassed about by a great cloud of witnesses.' And John, the Seer of Patmos, in vision beholds 'a multitude that no man could number, of all nations, and kindreds, and peoples and tongues' – the very fellowship of heaven itself.

106

Our *koinōnia*, then, is not confined to earth; it stretches 'within the veil'; it embraces both 'the saints on earth' and 'those whose work is done'. It binds together the Church Militant and the Church Triumphant, and its marching song is that of Charles Wesley:

> One family we dwell in Him,
> One Church, above, beneath.

Today that fellowship which began in Galilee with twelve men now numbers on earth a thousand millions. It is a fellowship called to be 'the working body of Christ' in the world, to live and labour and love in Christ's name, till it please God to wind up the scroll of history and consummate his great purpose of salvation.

Into that august fellowship you and I have been called. He who created it is still with us, through the Holy Spirit, with two hands held out, one to point the heavenward way, and the other to help us along. Looking down upon us is a mighty host who have fought the good fight and gone to their reward. Let us all strive in our day to be worthy – worthy of that great fellowship.

26

The Church

(Matt. 16.18)

What is the Church, the Church with a capital C? How parochial some of us tend to be in our thinking about it! We identify it with a building, inevitably our own stone-and-lime place of worship; or with our own denomination; or with a clerical class ('Here comes the Church', we say, as the clergyman comes along the road.) But the Christian Church – the *Ecclēsia* of God – is something incomparably bigger and older.

We may define it as *the new and true people of God, called into existence by God's saving action in Christ, and now numbering in the earth more than a thousand millions.* The great company of Christian people dispersed throughout the world – a supra-national divine society, embracing folk of every race and colour – this, and nothing less, is the Church Catholic, or Universal.

I

How did it come into being? The Christian church began when Christ called, trained, and sent out twelve men (the number, note, of the tribes in old Israel) to be the first-fruits of the Israel-to-be, the new 'chosen people' living under God's fatherly rule, the coming of which was the burden of Christ's Good News, and which he lived and died and rose again to create.

As all began in Galilee, so all culminated in Jerusalem with a cross on a hill and an empty tomb. And when, at the Last Supper, with broken bread and outpoured wine, Christ gave his men a share in the blessings of the 'new Covenant' foretold by the prophet Jeremiah, the Twelve sat round their master as the nucleus of the new people of God which, seven weeks later, on the day of Pentecost, was empowered for its high mission by the gift of the Holy Spirit.

During his earthly ministry Christ had named it his Father's 'little flock'. After Pentecost the young Church soon acquired new names, each reflecting some facet of the truth: 'the household of God', 'the bride of Christ', 'the fellowship of the Spirit'. But the Church's other and best-known name in the New Testament is 'the body of Christ'.

Why 'body'? A man's body is the instrument whereby he communicates with the external world. Now, as the book of Acts shows on page after page, the earliest Christians had a vivid sense of the living Christ present and working in their fellowship, through the Holy Spirit. So St Paul named the Church 'the (working) Body of Christ', that is, a social organism composed of many members, or limbs, and carrying out Christ's purposes in the world as once, in 'the days of his flesh', his physical body had done in Galilee and Judaea. (If you wish to go into the theology of this, study Paul's Epistle to the Ephesians.)

Christianity and Church, then, belong together, like Siamese twins. Some of us may have met people who claimed that they could be perfectly good Christians without joining the Church. This is a fallacy. (What should we say of a man who told us that he could be a perfectly good soldier without joining the Army?) Not for one moment does the New Testament support this view. What the apostles tell us is that to be a Christian is to be 'in Christ' (i.e., in faith-union with a living Lord), and this means being a member of the society of which Christ is the reigning head. As the notion of an unattached soldier is a nonsense, so is that of a 'maverick' Christian.

A man once said to the American evangelist D. L. Moody, 'I don't see that I can't be as good a Christian outside the Church as within it.' In answer, Moody stepped over to the fire, drew a burning coal from it with the tongs, and let it burn by itself. In silence the two men watched it smoulder and go out. 'I see,' said the man, and next Sunday went to church. The moral is obvious. All true Christian experience is experience gained, shared and matured in the fellowship of other Christians.

109

II

What, then, as the French say, is the Church's *raison d'être*, the reason for its existence? It is threefold.

First, to proclaim *'redemption's story'* (*as the hymn has it*) *and to offer up 'spiritual sacrifices of praise and prayer acceptable to God through Jesus Christ our Lord'* (*I Peter 2.5*).

This we do at public worship, which ought to be our joyful response to God for all that he is in his own glory and for all that he has done for us in Christ.

This the whole pattern of our worship should reflect, whether, as in the Old Testament lesson, the preparation in old Israel for the Gospel, or, as in the New Testament one, its fulfilment in Christ. So the sermon should bring a 'Word of God' to its hearers in their human predicament, be it sin, or sorrow, or despair. Finally, all our worship ought to end with the benedictory suggestion not just that we are being sent *away* but that we are being sent *out* to witness for the Gospel in the world.

So to the Church's second calling. We are saved into a society which has a mission to the whole world. The Church's role is therefore to be *God's collective missionary to men.* Today this mission is not confined to the heathen in foreign lands; it begins in the semi-pagan world around the Church's own doors. And here the witness of our own Christian lives will bear more effective testimony than many sermons.

Finally, the Church has a duty to apply her holy faith to public conduct by *providing a moral guide to society.* 'You are the salt of the earth,' Christ told his first disciples – 'salt', to keep society wholesome and preserve it from decay. So it should still be today. Many of the problems which vex mankind today are, at bottom, moral ones. In the New Testament we Christians have set before us standards of conduct far above those prevalent in the 'permissive society' around us – moral norms like the endurance of injuries without retaliation, magnanimity in judging other people, abstinence from sexual intercourse outside marriage, and deliberate self-denial for others' sake. On us as Christians lies the obligation not only to uphold these standards, but by our own lives to show whose we are and whom we seek to serve.

III

All this presents a daunting challenge to Christians in a world where today our society is sick and the Church's image tarnished. Worse still, she is sadly divided. How dare we sing, as we sometimes do, *fortissimo*:

> We are not divided,
> All one Body we,

when it is a plain and pathetic untruth? Nay more, what victory can await a religion whose regiments have on them the curse of the clans and go each its own way with pride, following a chief and losing a head?

How all these sects and schisms arose in Christendom is not for discussion here. The plain fact is that there are deep wounds in the body of Christ, and that this state of affairs accords neither with our Lord's prayer that 'they all may be one', nor with St Paul's teaching that 'there is one body and one Spirit'. Moreover, our unhappy divisions weaken the Church's witness at home, and perhaps even more abroad. How, for instance, do we answer converts from 'the Third World' when they ask us: 'Why cannot we sit together with all our Christian brothers at the Lord's Table?'

Happily in our times there has begun to blow through disunited Christendom a welcome 'wind of change'. It is called 'the Ecumenical Movement' (from the Greek *oikumenē*, which means 'the inhabited world'). Christians, so long content to shelter behind their own denominational barriers, have begun again to realize that God is calling them to recover their lost unity and present a common front to the world.

To be sure, ticklish problems of church order (e.g., women in the ministry and bishops in presbytery) still await settlement; but today the stress ought to be on the many things Christians hold in common rather than on those things which keep them apart. Nor should thorny doctrinal questions be allowed to hold up the task of achieving *a working unity* in which all Christians can cooperate to form what has been called 'a United States of the Church'.

111

Let us begin then at the grass roots, as some are now doing, with Protestants and Catholics working together at the parish level, for the common Christian good of the community. Protestants will rightly continue to contest Rome's claim to be the only true Church. Yet they might well take their marching orders from Angelo Roncalli, sometimes known as 'the good Pope John': 'Whenever I see a wall between Christians,' he said, 'I try to pull out a brick.'

Here is a 'Go and do thou likewise' for all of us who call Christ Lord and Saviour.

27

Baptism

(Matt. 28.19f.)

The Gospel of St Matthew ends with the commission of the risen Christ: 'All authority in heaven and on earth has been given me. Go ye therefore and make disciples of all nations, baptizing them in the name of the Father and of the Son and of the Holy Spirit, teaching them to observe all that I have commanded you; and lo, I am with you always, even to the end of the world.'

Today we fulfil his command. But what is really happening when we sprinkle water on a child in the name of the Father, the Son and the Holy Spirit?

It is a common delusion that baptism is the sacrament at which the baby 'gets its name'. Yet we all know that it is in fact the parents – perhaps after long domestic argument – who give the baby its name. We call a child's first name its Christian name because it has become customary to utter this name at baptism. Yet the sacrament would be just as valid if the name were never spoken. Properly understood, Christian baptism is something which goes much deeper. We come much nearer the truth when we call it a 'christening'. For Christian baptism has to do with Christ and all that he has done for us.

To understand this, we must go back to the story of Christ in the gospels. At the prelude to his ministry the most dramatic moment came when Christ went down into the waters of Jordan, along with a crowd of sinners, to be baptized by John. As the Servant Son of God, he was deliberately 'numbering himself with the transgressors' (Isa. 53.12). John's baptism, we read, was 'for the remission of sins' – but Christ was not conscious of sin. It was 'for repentance' – but Christ was repenting not for his own sins but for the sins of the many.

113

A like dramatic moment came near the end of his ministry when he told his disciples, 'I have a baptism to be baptized with, and how am I straitened till it be accomplished.' By this he meant his baptism not in water but in blood. He was thinking of the suffering and death that awaited him in Jerusalem when he would 'give his life as a ransom for many'. And on the first Good Friday it all came true. There, on the cross, by his Father's will, and out of love for sinners, he was himself baptized in 'death's cold sullen stream', as three days later he was to be raised by God's power from the dead.

When therefore we are baptized – whether we realize it or not – we are made to share in that *one great baptism* of Christ's which now, by the work of God's Holy Spirit, is made available for all who will. The whole purpose of our baptism is that we may be taken up into the virtue of all that Christ has done for us, and in order that, as Paul said, in union with our risen Lord we too may rise into 'newness of life'.

In baptism we become members of Christ's body, which is the church. We are named as Christ's, as it is the hope and prayer of those who present us for baptism that we shall grow up to be Christian men and women.

If this doctrine of Christian baptism should take some of us out of our spiritual depths, perhaps an illustration will make it clearer. Sometimes – though the custom is not now as common as it once was – at a child's baptism, his (or her) grandmother presents the baby with a christening mug which the child uses as soon as he is able to sit at table. Later a day comes when the child asks who gave him the mug. 'It was your grandmother,' comes the reply, 'who loved you as a little child.' 'Where is she now?' asks the child. 'She is dead,' they tell him, perhaps adding, 'Gone to be with the Good Man Above.' 'And she loved me before I could speak – as soon as I was born?' 'Yes.'

So love comes home to the child as a beautiful thing, a thing which was about his very beginning, and yet a thing that goes with the child every day. Well, the gift of the christening mug is Christian baptism. It is a sign and symbol of the divine love which died to redeem us.

114

II

Think, then, of the sacrament of baptism, first, as a *sign*, a sign which God makes effective through his Holy Spirit. 'God shows his love for us,' wrote St Paul, 'in that while we were yet sinners Christ died for us.' Of that prevenient love of God this sacrament is the sign. It declares that before we were even born, or thought of, Christ died and rose, by God's will, for the salvation of sinners. When, in his later life, Martin Luther was visited by doubts or difficulties, he used to say to himself, *Baptizatus sum*, that is, 'I have been baptized.' By this he meant that at his baptism all the powers of Christ's death and resurrection had been applied to his life and were still potent to dissipate his doubts and overcome his sin.

Next, baptism is a *door*. The purpose of a door is to admit. So baptism admits into Christ's fellowship, which is the church. It is our welcome into the family of God. At his baptism a child really becomes a member of the body of Christ. Later, when we talk of his 'joining' the church, he is but taking over for himself the responsibilities of church membership which years before his parents assumed on his behalf.

Finally, baptism is a *promise* – a promise by the parents that they will bring up their child 'in the knowledge and love of God and of his Son Jesus Christ our Lord'. Here not only the corporate but also the vicarious element in Christianity comes out clearly. Not only are we 'members one of another', but we can be helped and saved by the faith of others, as the paralysed man was healed through the agency of his four friends who brought him to Jesus (Mark 2.1–5).

Just so, God's forgiving love in Christ comes to most of us through our parents when they bring us to the baptismal font. When they take their 'baptismal vows' in the presence of the congregation, they promise so to order their lives and their homes that the new life imparted to the child in baptism may later find fulfilment when, reaching years of discretion, he confirms for himself the promises once made on his behalf.

A sign, a door, a promise – this is the threefold meaning of baptism. It is the sign of the divine love that died to redeem us, the door of entry into the household of God, and the promise by the parents that, so far as in them lies, their child shall grow up to be a Christian and fight the good fight of faith until, at last, God calls him home.

Note

Not a few good Christians known as 'Baptists' hold strongly that the sacrament should only be administered to adults on conscious profession of their faith. How, they ask, can babes in arms possibly understand what is happening to them at the baptismal font? Do not some in fact seem vocally to register their dissent?

Christians who are not Baptists agree that the church must provide baptism for those who, unchristened in childhood, as adults profess their faith in Christ as Lord and Saviour. Yet they also hold that infant baptism has behind it sound Christian warrant.

First, in New Testament times whole households were baptized, and these certainly included children. Second, in infant baptism it is *the parents' faith* that matters, as we have seen. And, third, baptism *unto* faith has as good a right in the principle of the Gospel where grace *precedes* faith as baptism *upon* faith.

'Suffer the little children to come unto me, and forbid them not,' said Christ himself. It cannot then be unchristian to cast the mantle of God's grace over a little child, provided that we also insist that his Christian initiation will not be complete until, grown to years of discretion, he confirms for himself, by public profession, the vows which his parents once took on his behalf.

28

The Lord's Supper

(I Cor. 11.23–26)

What are we doing when we observe the sacrament of the Lord's Supper or, as we usually say, take Communion?

Of all the answers ever given, none seems to me to get nearer the heart of the matter than that given by Principal David Cairns of Aberdeen in a letter which he wrote to an Anglican friend. The sacrament, he said, has three elements. It is at once a retrospect and a prophecy, with a renewal of the Covenant face to face. In other words, it has to do with a memory, a hope, and a presence.

Let us take each of these things in turn.

I

To begin with, the sacrament is a remembering. 'This do,' said Christ, 'in remembrance of me,' or, as the words might better be translated, 'for my recalling.'

Here it is important to get this business of remembering straight – biblically straight. When the Bible talks about remembering, it does not mean, as we commonly do, a mere idea in the mind – a pale, neutral, static memory. Biblical remembering is always realistic and dynamic. When we remember in the Bible's way, we bring something out of the past into the present – make it real and contemporaneous, so that it becomes once again living and actual and potent.

So it was with the Jewish family when they kept the feast of the Passover out of which our Lord's Supper was born. For the Hebrew, to remember was to be caught up again by a kind of corporate memory in the Exodus, that mighty act by which, centuries before, God had delivered his forefathers from Egyptian

117

bondage. Did not their Law say: 'In every generation each one of us should regard himself as though he himself had gone forth from Egypt'?

But now, as St Paul tells the Corinthians, 'our Passover has begun: the sacrifice is offered, Christ himself' (I Cor. 5.7). And what we Christians are called to is a like dynamic remembering of that second and mightier Exodus (Luke 9.31) by which, through cross and resurrection, God broke savingly into history, and set up his New Covenant – his 'new deal' for sinners. 'This cup,' said Christ as he handed it to his disciples, 'is the New Covenant (which long ago the prophet Jeremiah foresaw) sealed by my blood.'

'Were you there,' asks the negro spiritual, 'when they crucified my Lord?' If you and I remember aright, we are 'there'. The cross steps out of its frame in past history, and we re-enact the crisis of our redemption. We are 'there' with the disciples in the upper room on the night in which he was betrayed. We are 'there' with Mary his mother and the beloved disciple at the foot of the cross. We are there with the three women at the empty tomb on the first Easter morning, to hear again the glad tidings: 'He is not here; he is risen!'

II

But if we look back at Communion, we also look forward. Thus did Christ himself in the upper room. 'I shall not drink again of the fruit of the vine,' he said, 'until that day when I drink it new in the Kingdom of God' (Mark 14.25).

It is our Lord's *au revoir* to his faithful followers. Never again will he drink wine at an earthly meal. But he will drink it again in a new sort – a new kind – in the kingdom of his Father. His thoughts are on the eternal, the supernal, Kingdom, that 'sweet and blessed country the home of God's elect'. He is saying, 'I will not drink wine any more until I drink it with you in my Father's house.'

So too all our Lord's Suppers ought to have a heavenly 'forward look', should lift our thoughts to Christ's coming in the glory of his Father, to the Church Triumphant, and all the beatitude of heaven.

Some have called this Supper 'the iron ration' of the Christian soldier, fortifying him afresh to do battle with the world and all its evils. And so it is. But it is not less what we used in Scotland to call the 'arles' – the first instalment and pledge – of the perfect fellowship of heaven:

> Feast after feast thus comes and passes by,
> Yet, passing, points to the glad feast above,
> Giving sweet foretaste of the festal joy,
> The Lamb's great bridal feast of bliss and love.

III

Looking back and looking forward, memory and hope – but there is a third element in this sacrament which binds memory and hope together and which alone entitles us to call it as we do – communion. Let us rid our minds once and for all of the idea that this act is mainly one of commemoration. How can we have a memorial of one who is still alive, still our life? The Christ whom we confess is no mere figure in an old, old story. He is one who by his resurrection has become a living and ubiquitous Lord – a Christ who still comes, unseen but not unknown, through the Holy Spirit.

He it is who gives and blesses in this supper. The broken bread and the outpoured wine are his 'love-tokens to his body, which is the church', signs which really convey what they symbolize, because they deepen and confirm the saving relationship between the Redeemer and his redeemed. For in this sacrament, still keeping troth with us, Christ offers us afresh the fruit of his finished work – forgiveness and new life.

Yet the renewing of the Covenant is not his only. As we are his faithful followers, *we* renew it also. In this *sacramentum* – this sacred oath of allegiance which is what the word originally meant – as long ago the Roman soldier to his emperor, we engage ourselves afresh to him who is the high captain of our salvation.

What do we promise? We promise to follow ever more worthily in that discipleship to which he calls us. We promise to be better and truer members of his 'working' body, which is the church.

119

We promise to fight ever more bravely under his banner to our life's end.

Therefore, when you sit at the holy table, look back – to the cross and resurrection. Look forward – to the perfect fellowship of heaven. And renew your vows to Christ your Lord and Saviour who now meets you in this sacrament with his grace.

29

The Christian Ethic

(Rom. 12)

When the preacher reminded his congregation that the Gospel had a 'behaving' as well as a 'believing' side to it, he was referring to the Christian ethic.

Ethic (or ethics) is the science of morals, and, like other sciences, there is more than one variety of it. Thus, those people who find no place in their thinking for the supernatural, opt, naturally enough, for 'naturalistic ethics', for 'morals without religion'. But for Christians who believe in a 'bigger world', transcending this one, yet interpenetrating it, the moral imperative, the 'Thou shalt', comes from beyond, from God as he has revealed himself in Christ. In other words, Christian behaviour, according to Christ and his apostles, is our human response in living to the grace of God. 'In the New Testament,' said Erskine of Linlathen, 'religion is grace and ethics is gratitude.'

I

Long before Christ came the Greek philosophers had of course given grave thought to the question of 'the good life', and had come up with their answer: *Mēden agan*, 'nothing in excess', all things in moderation. The Christian ethic, however, derives not from Aristotle and the Greeks but from Christ and his apostles, like Paul and John. Moreover, though it presupposes the Ten Commandments given to old Israel, it goes beyond them, as the Sermon on the Mount shows.

First, it makes agapē, or Christian love, the master-key of morals. Unlike our word 'love' today – which can mean almost everything from Hollywood to Heaven – *agapē* is neither erotic nor sentimental. Study Christ's teaching about it, and you cannot but note how practically and all-embracingly he construes the verb 'to love'. By 'loving' he means 'caring', caring actively and selflessly not only for the decent and the deserving, but for all who need our help, even enemies. By 'love' he means total devotion to the other man in his need, as his tale about the Good Samaritan shows. 'Christianity,' said Baron von Hügel to his niece on his death-bed, 'Christianity taught us to care. Caring is the greatest thing. Caring matters most.' Is not this what Christ tells us in his Sermon on the Mount and St Paul in I Cor. 13?

Yet this is but half of 'love's story' in the Gospels. If, in his ministry, Christ called for such selfless caring, by his death he gave the word 'love' a still richer meaning. There, at Calvary, the supreme act of *agapē* had been performed. 'God,' as St Paul wrote, 'shows his own love for us, in that while we were yet sinners Christ died for us.'

So, as A. C. Craig has said, 'the word love always needs a dictionary, and for us Christians the dictionary is Jesus Christ. He took this chameleon of a word and gave it a fast colour, so that ever since it is lustred by his teaching and life, and dyed in the crimson of Calvary, and shot through with the sunlight of Easter morning.'

Here it is worth pausing to make a point about Christian love When St John tells us that 'God is love', he does not mean that loving is but one of God's many activities. He means that *all* God's activity is loving activity. If he creates, he creates in love; if he rules, he rules in love; if he judges, he judges in love. In short, all God does is the expression of his nature, which is to 'love'.

Now 'we love, because he first loved us'. Our Christian love is really God's love to us in Christ reflected and responded to. So, when St Augustine sums up the Christian love-ethic as 'Love God, and do what you like', or, more accurately translated, 'Love, and what you will, do', what he means is: 'If you hold your peace, through love hold your peace; if you cry out, through love cry out; if you correct, through love correct; if you spare, through love spare.' All our Christian activity, whether protesting, rebuking, sparing, or, on occasion, just keeping our mouths shut – is, or ought to be, loving activity.

Still today, in a world so very different from that of Christ and his apostles, such love ought to be the law of the Christian's every-day living. Hard it will often be to apply in our complex society; but, as we seek to practise it, we shall find that it has a capacity to sweeten human relations and make life's rough places plain which nothing else has.

II

In the second place, *the Christian ethic combines gladness in hardship with the promise of heavenly reward.* Is not this the theme which keeps sounding through Christ's recipes for happiness, which we call 'the Beatitudes'?

(Here, to forestall the moralist's objection that 'virtue should be its own reward', let us note that Christ promises a heavenly reward to those who are obedient without thought of reward. 'Do good,' he is recorded as saying, 'expecting nothing in return' (Luke 6.35) – a point driven unforgettably home in his parable of the Last Judgment.)

Now this note of 'gladness in hardship' was something new and wonderful, as down the centuries since it has characterized great Christians from Paul onwards. In the Middle Ages none better embodied this virtue than St Francis of Assisi. Joyousness in poverty was the saint's life-style. 'For the love of Christ,' he said, 'bear willingly and gladly every affliction that shall befall thee.'

And if we look for a modern parallel, is there a better one than Dr Edward Wilson of Antarctic fame, that 'Mr Standfast' who, from the tent of death, wrote thus to his wife: 'Don't be unhappy. All is for the best. We are playing a good part in a great scheme arranged by God himself, and all is well.'

III

The third feature of the Christian ethic in the New Testament is that, *for its practice, it presupposes a fresh gift of divine power, the Pentecostal gift.*

Sometimes in the New Testament epistles, it is called the Holy Spirit, and sometimes it is the living Christ. It is a distinction without a real difference, for the presence of the Holy Spirit is really Christ's own presence in spirit.

For Christians, then, Christ is 'the Lord of all good life': yet not simply as the past embodiment in human life of perfect goodness. Ours is a living Lord who 'abides the same yesterday, today and for ever'. He it is who still today leads us on our pilgrim way, as in faith-union with him we find strength for the journey. Still, in this twentieth century, this Christ, as T. W. Manson phrased it, has two hands, one to point the way, the other held out to help us along, as we have his own assurance that he will be with us 'to the end of the world'.

<h1 style="text-align:center">IV</h1>

Space will not allow us to dwell on other features of Christ's moral teaching: for example, its inwardness ('from within, out of the heart'), or to show how he gave a new glory to the idea of humble service.

Today our problem is how to apply these Gospel ethics to situations which never came within the purview of Christ and his apostles. Thus, if the New Testament does give us guidance on the normal attitude of Christians to the civil powers (see, for example, Rom. 13.1–7), it has little or nothing to say on the controversy between pacifists and non-pacifists or the problem of 'the just war'. (Christ's 'love your enemies' refers to personal antagonists.)

The task before us today is therefore one of seeking, with the Gospel ethics before us and the help of the Holy Spirit, to work out Christian solutions to the moral problems of our day. For the church has a right and duty to translate her holy faith into ethics relevant to the world we live in, as she has also a right and duty to cry out, like Amos and other Old Testament prophets, against the evils which disfigure our society.

Yet protests, by themselves, are not enough. What is needed is some positive form of Christian action. What then should be the church's strategy in this holy war?

What we need, say some, is a Christian political party like those on the Continent calling themselves 'Christian Democrats'. If some of us cannot accept this view, it is for two good reasons. First, no political set-up can ever be equated with the Kingdom of God. And, second, no man's piety or personal holiness is a guarantee of his political sagacity.

There is another and better way. The church's prime duty is not to solve 'the social problem', whatever form it takes, but to *provide the men, the principles and the public* which can. Her aim should be to turn out men and women who, adding Christian conviction to their own professional expertise in business, industry and politics, will carry Christian cleanness of hand and purpose into the places where today the real power lies and the big decisions are taken. So best will the church fulfil her task of bringing Christian principle into the world around her and prove herself 'the moral guide to society' which she ought to be.

30

The Faith of our Fathers

(Ps. 22.4; Heb. 12.1f.)

Our spiritual advisers tell us that what we ought to possess is a personal faith. 'Don't be content', they counsel us, 'to take your faith second-hand, from your parents. Get one of your ownest own, and live by it.'

No doubt they are right. A faith of our own is the kind needed for the day when 'life tumbles in'. Nevertheless, it is not the whole truth. For what if a man loses that faith of his own? What if tragedy and sorrow conspire to shake his former faith to its very foundations? Why, then is the time to live by the faith of your fathers. If you cannot say with doubting Thomas, 'My Lord and my God', you can at least say 'The God of my fathers'. To be sure, the faith of our fathers can never be a permanent substitute for a faith of our own. But what a reinforcement it can be when,

> Troubles rise, and dangers frown,
> And days of darkness fall.

And if, in the desperate hour, when all the black devils of doubt are clutching at your throat, you can say with the Psalmist:

> Our fathers trusted in thee;
> They trusted, and thou didst deliver them',

then, clinging to the faith of others, you may stay afloat in the storm till rescue comes.

I

First, then, remember that *our faith is no new, untried venture.* 'We come unto our fathers' God.' Down the centuries the Christian faith has sustained and fortified countless millions from Nero's day to Hitler's, and often in the certainties of yesterday we may find solid ground amid the uncertainties of today.

This is the message of the famous eleventh chapter of Hebrews. The author was writing to put courage into Christians faced with persecution. How does he do it? By reciting to them the roll-call of the heroes of faith, from the patriarchs to the Maccabees: all their great forefathers who 'had endured as seeing him who is invisible'. 'Wherefore,' he concludes, 'seeing we are compassed about with so great a cloud of witnesses, let us run with patience the race that is set before us, ever looking to Jesus, the pioneer and perfecter of our faith, who for the joy that was set before him endured the cross, despising the shame, and is now seated at the right hand of the throne of God.' In other words, let the faltering faith of the living strengthen itself by the faith of the dead, and, above all, by the faith of him who 'was dead, and is now alive for evermore'.

Now this can be our way too. When the lamp of our own faith burns low, we can remember all those fine, brave, good souls – fathers, mothers, friends – who walked steadfastly through this house of their pilgrimage and went down at the last into the dark valley unafraid, because they knew that the great Shepherd of the sheep was there with them.

We are upheld, then, by unseen hands. Behind us stretch more than sixty generations of faithful Christian men and women. And therefore we have a right to say with the Psalmist:

> We have heard with our ears, O God,
> Our fathers have told us,
> What deeds Thou didst perform in their days,
> In the days of old.

II

If the first point to remember is that 'our faith is no new untried venture', the second one is that *we ought to make far more of this than we do.*

Of one failing we Protestants have often been guilty, viz., that of turning our religion into 'an individualist salvation by private

127

bargain', when what Christ wrought was rescue for a whole world of sinners. True Christianity is far more than a purely personal transaction between the believer and his God. It is nothing if not *social*. The Christian takes his place in a society which goes back nearly twenty centuries and now numbers more than a thousand millions in the world. Ours is no upstart faith – like, say, the communists'. We can say,

> We are travelling home to God
> In the way our fathers trod,

Yes, and their fathers and forefathers.

Of course, in small ways, most of us remember this truth. For example, a son like Thomas Carlyle gratefully recalls what his mother's faith had meant to him. 'O pious, kind mother,' he writes in his diary, 'good, brave and truthful soul as ever I have known, your poor Tom, long out of his schooldays now, has fallen very lonely, very lame and broken in this pilgrimage of his . . . But, from your grave in Ecclefechan yonder you bid him trust in God, and that also he will try and do.'

Then we realize how much this great man owed to the faith of Margaret Aitken, his mother.

Yet there is more to it than this. This Christian faith of ours is one that has had to stand the tests and shocks of almost two thousand years. So when today its enemies, in press or on television, turn their weapons on it, let us remember, for our comfort, the saying of Tertullian, the African church father, 'The faith is an anvil that has worn out many hammers.'

In Switzerland, I am told, your mountain guide will often cut on his alpenstock the names of the high peaks he has conquered with its help. Just so, like that staff, our faith has supported countless great men and women down the centuries. It is the faith of Paul and Augustine, of Columba and Francis of Assisi, of Luther and John Knox, of John Bunyan and John Wesley, of Samuel Johnson and Walter Scott, of Mary Slessor and Mother Teresa, of Lord Reith of the BBC and Lord Montgomery of Alamein. And the mere recalling of these noble names ought to put heart into us when the cable of our own faith shows signs of slipping in the night of fear.

128

III

But – and this is the clinching consideration – *the greatest fortifier of our faith is the Lord Jesus himself.*

You and I believe in God through him, and not least through the example of his own faith.

In his letter to the Galatians, St Paul, according to the Authorized Version, writes: 'The life which I now live in the flesh I live by the faith *of* the Son of God, who loved me, and gave himself for me.' Now, if you like, the AV here mistranslates the original Greek which means not 'the faith *of* the Son of God' but (as in the RSV and NEB) 'faith *in* the Son of God'.

Yet the mistranslation contains truth, the truth expressed in Thomas Lynch's fine hymn:

> I have a Captain, and the heart
>   Of every private man
> Has drunk in valour from his eyes
>   Since first the war began.

You and I run our race, remembering not only 'the great cloud of witnesses' referred to in Hebrews, but that 'Captain', Jesus Christ himself. Have you, dear reader, ever stopped to think what a terrific strain the cross must have put on his own faith? 'Jesus the Saviour reigns', we sing in church; yes, but through what agony and desolation of spirit the Victor went to his heavenly throne! Surely, if to any man it is given by his own faith to save others, that power is his who knew the agony of Gethsemane and the dreadful dereliction of the cross.

Men and women, there are always people who find it hard to find meaning in the old creeds. They want to believe, but the candle of their faith gutters in the black night of doubt. Then perhaps only one thing will help them – 'looking to Jesus'. 'I believe in God – the Father – Almighty'. This was his faith as his crucifiers drove the nails into his living flesh. Through him, it may be yours also, today and all the days of your life.

> Our fathers trusted in thee:
> They trusted, and thou didst deliver them.

In that faith, the faith of your fathers and of the Son of God himself, I bid you go forward into the future.

31

The Gospel for a Secular World

(John 17.16–18)

'They are not of the world as I am not of the world . . . As thou didst send me into the world, so have I sent them into the world.' We are listening to part of Christ's prayer of consecration for his disciples in the upper room 'on the night in which he was betrayed'. Not of the world, his disciples' future mission will nonetheless lie in it. And before he goes out to Gethsemane, he commends them to his heavenly Father.

Now for St John (whose Gospel we have been quoting) 'the world' bears a quite distinctive sense. It means 'human society as it organizes itself apart from God', mankind mobilized in defiance of the divine purpose. Roughly it corresponds to the secularized world in which we are living today – the world of sex and violence, 'mods and rockers', nuclear bombs and 'morals without religion'. And I think we might profitably consider what this secularized world really is, how we ought to present the Gospel to it, and what the church's role in this ought to be.

I

The 'secularized world', then, is that world which, on the one hand, has broken with traditional morality and belief, and which, on the other hand, looks to modern science and technology – computers, micro-chips, and so on – to solve most of mankind's problems.

But, if we left it at that – were concerned only with the boons and bestowals of modern science – we should have described only one side of the medal; and an honest look at the dark side might well make us gravely pause. The sober truth is that this 'brave new world' of ours is, as T. S. Eliot said, one which 'advances progressively backwards'. For, along with its repudiation of traditional morality like the Ten Commandments, and its scientific advances, of which the most horrific is the nuclear bomb, it has brought the mass of people not peace of mind but a certain nameless fear and foreboding and often a bleak sense of the futility and meaninglessness of life. Indeed, where the secularizing process has gone furthest, the suicide rate has rocketed alarmingly, astrology has prospered, and mental illness increased almost beyond the power of medical science to cope with it.

Does not all this point to one conclusion, the failure of this secularized society to satisfy the deepest spiritual needs of men – to fill what has been called 'the God-shaped blank' in the human heart? Long ago the wise man said, 'Where there is no vision, the people perish,' or, as the Revised Standard Version translates it, 'the people cast off restraint'. And I have no doubt that, if the apostle Paul were among us today, he would diagnose the malaise of our modern society as a divine nemesis on a generation which had turned away from what he calls 'God's way of righting wrong', in order to worship idols like sex, power, money and the like.

II

Such is our human situation today. What then should be our strategy as Christians in it?

First, we must not turn our backs on this secular world and retreat into our ecclesiastical bolt-holes. On the contrary, as God is the Lord of history, we must believe that this secularizing process is part of his purpose and therefore to be accepted.

Second, we must seek to present the Gospel to it in ways modern men can understand, avoiding obsolete religious jargon and trying to use idioms and images which will come home to men and women who are better briefed in the rules of Bingo than in the precepts of the Bible.

What we must *not* do is to copy those *avant garde* Christians who invite us to accommodate the Gospel to the temper of the times, who bid us cry 'Glory to man in the depths of his being' instead of 'Glory to God in the highest', who would substitute 'Jesus the Man for others' for 'Thou art the Christ, the Son of the living God', and for whom 'faith' becomes 'existential self-understanding', not, as in the New Testament, a taking of God at his Word in Christ.

All this may be intelligible to modern man – though I gravely doubt it – but it is not New Testament Christianity. (Thus, when some of us seek God 'in the depth of our being' what we find is not God but original sin.) In fine, if the price of making the Gospel palatable to modern man is its perversion, we should refuse to pay it and be content, like Paul, to be 'fools for Christ's sake'.

III

Turn now from the Gospel to the church. What ought to be the role of the church in this secularized world? Is it God's will that it should be merely an ark of refuge from the snares and seductions of the wicked world outside? Or is it his will that the church should be a kind of task-force, going out into the world to witness for Christ and to serve men in love for his sake? Surely the answer is not in doubt. Listen to Christ himself: 'You are the salt of the earth. You are the light of the world. Behold, I send you forth.' God raised up the church to fulfil a mission in it, not apart from it. And the church becomes truly the church when, scorning to be merely a rest-camp for the faithful, it goes militantly on the march; when, refusing to be just Christ's 'mystical' body, it becomes his 'working body in the world.

Time was when many of us saw the task of the church and its ministry rather differently. Essentially her role was to persuade men to accept Christ as Saviour and Lord, so that repentant, baptized and confirmed they might go on growing in holiness, and at last be shepherded safely into their eternal home. I dare not say that this is no part of the church's task today; but if we conceive it *only* in this way, are we not blind to its dominical *raison d'être*, and disobedient to our risen Lord's commandment to his first followers: 'Go ye therefore and make disciples of all nations'?

Happily there are not wanting signs that, under the Holy Spirit's guidance, Christians are realizing anew that the church's task is not merely to save men out of the world but to equip men to do God's work in it.

133

IV

One final question. How ought we, as committed Christians, to live in this secularized world?

Dietrich Bonhoeffer, greatest of modern Christian martyrs, had no doubt about the answer. He was convinced that for secular modern man the word 'religion' all too often meant either renouncing the world, or the selfish pursuit of one's own salvation. So he called for 'religionless Christianity' and the Christian's radical involvement in the world's life. God, he kept saying, is not a Sunday God, a religious God, a churchly God. The God and Father of our Lord Jesus Christ is the God of the every day and the whole of life. Nor was it otherwise with him whom we call his Son. While Jesus lived on earth, he was not a conventionally religious man: he was, as the Jewish churchmen bitterly complained, 'the friend of publicans and sinners', the man who went out of his way to fraternize with the godless. And so it should be today for us who confess Christ as Saviour and Lord.

Bonhoeffer was right. No deliberate seeking of a sheltered life can be called truly Christian. Ever since Christ's critics called him 'a gluttonous man and a winebibber' true Christianity has never been world-renouncing. On the contrary, it has claimed the whole of life and the world for God.

Yet Bonhoeffer's call to 'Christian worldliness' must never be taken to mean that the Christian must so immerse himself in the life of the wider world that he neglects the discipline of 'the inner room' (Matt. 6.6) which means private daily prayer, and the regular use of the sacrament of the Lord's Supper. Without these all talk of Christian worldliness is vain.

Here, as elsewhere, we take our example from our Lord himself. Jesus, as the Gospels tell us, regularly went apart into solitary places to pray, not in order that he might withdraw altogether from the world, but in order that he might the better do God's work in it. Should it not be the same with us his followers? If from time to time we draw apart from the world, it is in order that, in communion with God, we may the better know his will, and go out into the world to do it. We come aside in worship, or we keep the holy tryst of the Lord's Supper, precisely in order that we may be sent out, not to live united with God apart from the world but to live in it as the sign and first-fruit of God's uniting of the world to himself in Jesus Christ.

32

'This is life eternal'

(John 17.3)

What is time? What is eternity? Down the centuries many wise heads have pondered these questions. We know that we are creatures of time, and we believe that God belongs to eternity. Our years come and go. God's years do not. If then we are creatures of time, can we know anything about God's eternity?

John, the fourth evangelist, is sure we can. He believes he has found the secret of eternal life, and he wants to share it with others. Indeed, it is for this very purpose (he tells us) he has written his book. What then does he mean by eternal life?

I

The first point to grasp is that there is a difference between 'eternal life' and 'everlasting life'. Everlasting life describes a life that simply goes on and on for ever, like Tennyson's brook. Eternal life is a matter of quality rather than of quantity. It is life of a new kind, life carried into a new dimension, life with the tang of eternity about it.

Moreover – and this is his second point – this new kind of life can begin even here and now. 'This is life eternal,' he writes, not, 'This will be.'

But eternity – God's time, here in this fallen world of ours – how can this be possible?

Start then with a familiar experience. Suppose you are spending the evening in the company of congenial friends. While it lasts, that time of perfect fellowship, and your enjoyment of it is steady, all awareness of the past or the future simply falls away. You are lost in an enjoyment that is all present. When, at the end of it, glancing at your watch, you find it is well past mid-

136

night, you say, 'My goodness! I never noticed the time passing.' Precisely. In that simple experience you have somehow got above time.

Take a second illustration, this time from music. The composer Mozart has described for us his method of composing. He tells how, in his imagination, he could hear his symphonies 'all at once' – simultaneously. 'I don't hear the notes one after another, as they are later to be played,' he explained, 'but it is as if, in my fancy, they were all at once.' And he goes on to tell of the happiness this experience has brought him. 'The actual hearing of the whole together,' he says, 'is the best gift I have to thank my divine master for.' Was this one of the reasons, I wonder, why I remember the great theologian Karl Barth saying at an Oxford conference, 'If there is to be music in heaven, it will be Mozart'?

Now take the last and greatest example of what we have been considering.

Shortly after his conversion to the faith, St Augustine and his saintly mother Monica were spending one fine evening at Ostia, near Rome. And, as they talked together about the deep things of God, Augustine was vividly aware that they had left time behind, or got above it. 'Still higher did we climb,' he says, 'by the staircase of the Spirit, thinking and speaking of Thee, and marvelling at thy works, O God. And as we talked and yearned, we touched the life for an instant with the full force of our hearts.'

So deep, so intense, was the joy of that time that Augustine felt that, if it could have been prolonged, it would be the very life of heaven itself.

Here, then, we may understand how eternity can somehow enter time, and man can somehow experience it in advance. Now we may begin to perceive what St John meant when he wrote: 'This is life eternal.'

II

But what is this eternal life, really? St John answers: 'It is knowing thee the only true God, and Jesus Christ whom thou hast sent.' Here the original Greek is even plainer: 'Eternal life means getting to know thee, the only real God.' Its secret is a growing acquaintance with the only real God, and this is to be had by getting to know Jesus Christ who is God's messenger to us men.

What does knowing God mean? Does it mean taking a degree in divinity or mastering many stout volumes of theology? If this were so, most of us would be doomed to life-long ignorance of God. Happily, it means something much simpler, much deeper.

For an illustration. There is all the difference in the world between 'knowing' and 'knowing about'. Thus, a five-year-old boy may 'know' his mother better than a twenty-year-old one whose knowledge of his mother's make-up, mental and physical, is much greater – may 'know' her far better in her essential motherliness. Just so, a simple peasant or fisherman may 'know' God better than a learned theologian who can discourse about God's existence and his attributes.

By 'knowing' God, St John means gaining personal experience of God, getting to 'know' him as one person gets to know another in what has been called a personal 'I-Thou' relationship, such as is described in the great 139th Psalm: 'O Lord, thou hast searched me and known me.' So, says St John, the secret of eternal life is very simple. It lies in getting to know God through Christ. God dwells in his heaven, but in Christ he has come into our world in order that we may know him as a child knows his father. Eternal life is getting to know God as he has revealed himself in Christ his Son, that Son who said, 'No one comes to the Father but by me.'

One day, last century, that fine Christian layman, Thomas Erskine of Linlathen, met a shepherd in the hills, and, the talk turning to belief in God, asked him, 'Do you know the Father?' The shepherd went away sadly, for he could not answer. Years later, when the two men met again, the shepherd took the first word, 'I know the Father now.'

III

To sum up what we have been saying. Eternal life is a life of growing acquaintance with an unseen heavenly Father; a life of which the living Christ, who now comes to us, unseen but not unknown, through the Holy Spirit, is the Mediator, a life con-

138

tinually spending itself in love yet never diminished. In short, a life of fellowship – with God who gives it, with Christ who mediates it, with the brethren who share it. 'All this, and heaven too.' For, if we may experience eternal life in foretaste here on earth, only beyond death shall we enjoy it in its fullness. Then knowledge will turn to sight, and in that sight and in the company of the redeemed will come the full flowering of the new life we begin here and now.

Is it not time that we Christians thought more about these things than we do? Immersed in the stream of time, busied with getting and spending, all concerned to build our welfare states and paradises on earth, we need to remember that our highest and holiest hopes lie otherwhere; that even now we may begin to taste that eternal life which God has reserved in its plenitude, for those who love him, beyond the bourne of death; and that the secret of it all lies in getting to know the only real God whose name is Father – knowing him through Christ who is God's messenger to lead us home to him:

> In the hour of death, after this life's whim,
> When the heart beats low and the eyes grow dim,
> And pain has exhausted every limb,
> The lover of the Lord shall trust in him.

> For even the purest delight may pall,
> And power must fail, and the pride must fall,
> And the love of the dearest friends grow small,
> But the glory of the Lord is all in all.

33

The Higher Hope

(Rom. 4.18)

We talk about 'hoping against hope'. Who was it first 'hoped against hope'? It was the patriarch Abraham. 'In hope,' we read, 'he believed against hope.' When, humanly speaking, everything seemed against what he hoped for – the birth of a son to himself and Sarah when they seemed too old to have a family – Abraham kept on hoping. Against the lower hope he believed in the higher hope, and, by and by, with the birth of Isaac, his hoping was rewarded.

What is this higher hope?

Suppose the morning dawns with leaden skies and the rain falling from apparently inexhaustible clouds. One man goes to the window, casts one glance at the heavens, and comes back shaking his head. 'It's no good,' he says, 'the rain is on for all day.' But the other man refuses to be cast down by mere appearances. He has heard perhaps, from the weather-men, that there is fine weather following in the wake of the rain, or he knows that the wind sits in the wrong quarter for a continuous downpour. So he refuses to be discouraged, makes ready for a fair day, and by and by the clouds roll away and King Sol shines out in all his glory.

Now this is not a weather forecast for today; but it is an example of the higher hope in the natural world. And we shall see that, as in the natural world, so also in the spiritual, there are two levels of hope – a higher and a lower. The man who stands on the lower level builds his hope on the surface facts and appearances. The man who stands on the other level builds his hope on the deeper facts and on the character of things.

Two kinds of hope there are, then, and men are quick to

140

distinguish between them. The first sort, since they can so easily grasp it, they call shrewd and sensible. The other they dismiss as far-fetched and forlorn. Yet, in the event, it is this second sort of hope that is often justified.

For example. Pharaoh and the Egyptians watch Moses and his little band of Hebrew slaves setting out from the land of bondage. What lies before them? Nothing apparently but the pitiless desert sands and the Red Sea. One end, and one end only. But the man Moses does not think so. He has heard a call from higher places, and out he pushes into the unknown, convinced that God will bring his people to the promised land. And so, in the end, it comes to pass.

Now come down thirteen centuries and consider another man sustained by this higher hope. But, looking at him, this little tent-maker from Tarsus, you would never guess it. No one watching Paul set out to win the great Gentile world for Christ would have dreamt that he had the remotest chance of success. All human odds seem stacked against him. Ah, but this man is living in the higher hope. He knows that God has called him to be the apostle to the Gentiles, and out into that 'hard pagan world' he goes to do a work beside which, as Lord Birkenhead said, the achievements of Alexander the Great and of Napoleon pale into insignificance – this little man who wrote the very words of our text, who 'against hope believed in hope'.

Oh, I grant you that this higher hope does sound unreasonable and unrealistic – until you consider what it really is. And when you do, you find that, so far from flying in the face of reason, it is simply a reasonable confidence in a higher power – confidence in God who is the lord of history and who has revealed his saving grace in Jesus Christ his Son.

II

Now let us see how this higher hope can transform your life and mine.

Take first the problem of besetting sin. You know, as I do, what a strangle-hold such sin can get on you. You try and try, by yourself, to break with it, and always you fail. Left to your own resources, you are impotent. Only a higher power can help

141

you. And have you not just such a power in Christ – the living Christ who still comes today through the Holy Spirit? If you can turn to him as your unseen helper, saying, 'Christ helping me, I will break with this sin', it shall be possible for you to hope in him, and to prevail – to rise on stepping stones of your old self into 'newness of life'. Down nineteen centuries countless men and women have proved it can be done.

Or apply this higher hope to the world in which we are living: the world of violence and vandalism, of corruption and pollution, of racial tensions and 'cold wars', the world in which the super-powers stand glowering at each other from behind their stock-piled nuclear weapons . . .

Consider all these things; and, if you live by the lower hope, you must often succumb to despair. From such despair only the higher hope, born of a firm Christian faith, can deliver you. That faith has never shut its eyes to the giant power of evil, or harboured the illusion that man is naturally good. But it has never ceased to proclaim – and here lies the source of its higher hope – that this world, for all its sinning, belongs to God, that God has given his own Son for its saving, and that, as God is God, he must finally vanquish all evil. This is the rock of truth which we call the Gospel, and when your feet are on that rock, you can exult even in the whirlpool.

Or take the supreme crisis which can assail any individual's faith.

One bitter day death lays his hand on one who was dearer to you than life. As you lay the body of that loved one in the grave, a mocking voice within you seems to whisper, 'The book is closed – now and for ever.' Thus confronted by the Great Leveller, what has the man to say who lives only by the lower hope? No more than, in the first century BC, the Roman poet Catullus said to his sweetheart Lesbia:

> Setting suns may rise in glory;
> But when little life is o'er,
> There's an end to all the story –
> We shall sleep, and wake no more.

Beautiful? Yes, but how unspeakably hopeless! How different

was the assurance, just one century later, which Paul gave to his converts:

But now is Christ risen from the dead and become the first fruits of those who have fallen asleep. For, as in Adam all die, so also, in Christ, shall all be made alive. Therefore sorrow not as those who have no hope. For, since we believe that Jesus died and rose again, even so, through Jesus, will God bring with him those who have fallen asleep; and so we shall be for ever with the Lord.

Yes, that is Paul, the man who lived by the higher hope, who 'against hope believed in hope'.

Here, then, is a watchword for all Christians, to carry them through not only the despairs and dangers of the day but all the chances and changes that life holds. Live by that hope; labour in that hope; and, when your time comes, die in it. O, never a fear that it will disappoint you; for it is built on the God and Father of our Lord Jesus Christ, who is our hope – our hope for this world and for that which is to come.

34

The Holy City

(Rev. 21.2)

There are some people who, when they get a new book, cannot resist the temptation to read the last chapter first, to see how it all will end. Nor are they altogether to be blamed if their book is the last one in the Bible, the Revelation of St John the Divine, as the Authorized Version styles him. (A better name for him would be 'John the Seer of Patmos' – Patmos, that rocky isle in the Aegean Sea where the Romans had imprisoned him for his unyielding loyalty to the Christian faith.)

His book, which is all about the judgment and victory of God, has been well likened to 'a tunnel' with light at the beginning (chapters 1–5) and light at the ending (chapters 21–22.5), and, in the middle, 'a long stretch of darkness through which lurid objects thunder past, bewildering and stunning the reader'.

In these long middle stretches (chapters 6–20) we have indeed 'the devil's own plenty' of darkness and doom, of plagues, conflagrations and catastrophes, of dragons, beasts and monsters of the pit. But, when at length we grope our way to the end of the tunnel, suddenly, with chapter 21, the world of the past is gone, and there breaks on our view the splendour of a new creation.

Transported by the Spirit of God to a mountain-top, St John sees 'the holy city, the new Jerusalem, coming down from God out of heaven, as beautiful as a bride dressed for her husband'. It shone, he tells us, with 'all the radiant glory of God'. Twelve gates it had, each of them a pearl, with on it the name of one of the tribes of Israel. Its wall, which towered fifteen hundred miles high, had written on its foundation stones the names of the twelve apostles. And the city itself, a marvel of pure gold, had the shape of a cube (for the ancients, the pattern of perfection). Through the streets of the city flowed the river of the water of life, with, on either bank, the tree of life whose leaves were for the healing of the nations. And the vision of the New Jerusalem culminates in a glimpse of God and the Lamb enthroned in glory, the worship of the church triumphant, and the sound of a Hallelujah chorus.

Yet this grand finale is not altogether unprepared for. All through those preceding visions of judgment, St John, by means of his wonderful 'interludes' – the vision of the redeemed martyrs in glory, the triumph-song of Moses and the Lamb, and the nuptials of the Lamb and his bride (which is the church) – has been giving us fore-glimpses of the glories of heaven. At last, in chapter 21, having described the final battle between the armies of heaven and the legions of hell, and the last judgment, St John, like a new Moses, stands on his own Mount Pisgah, and surveys for us the promised land, 'the home of God's elect'.

II

Nineteen hundred years separate us from the Seer of Patmos. What are we Christians nowadays to make of his 'Pisgah view' of Paradise?

Time was when our pious forefathers regarded these last two chapters of Revelation as a divinely-inspired ordnance map of Paradise, a topography of Heaven. If we no longer indulge in this celestial geographizing, it is because we now know better how to interpret St John's trance-like visions and his mystic numbers (three is the number of heaven, four of earth; twelve is the church number, as seven is the perfect number). John's interest lies in symbols rather than in statistics, and his true purpose in these chapters is to depict, if possible, the magnitude and perfection of the eternal city. This is why he almost bursts the bonds of language to describe the indescribable and suggest, in Wordsworth's phrase,

> Glory beyond all glory ever seen
> By waking sense or by the dreaming soul.

Accordingly, St John's priceless legacy to Christendom has not been his apocalyptic architectonics but his evocative images of what Christ himself called 'my Father's house'. And it is not the celestial map-makers but the Christian poets who have best caught his meaning and used his mystic visions to instruct Christian piety and kindle Christian hope, whether it be the anonymous Song of Mary, 'Hierusalem, my happy home', or St Bernard's 'Jerusalem the Golden', or Adelaide Procter's 'Holy City', that sacred ballad dear to many Victorians.

Can they still do this for us today, when men are much more interested in the 'secular' city than the 'holy' one, and when a modern Christian prophet, Reinhold Niebuhr, has wisely warned us that we should not not 'claim any knowledge of either the furniture of heaven or the temperature of hell'? Must we now mournfully dismiss John's vision as but the fantasy of an overwrought oriental imagination utterly incredible to occidental Christians in a scientific age?

III

In answer, two things must be said, one general and the other particular.

First, *all our Christian ideas about the last things are basically transpositions into the key of the hereafter of that revelation of God which is already ours in Christ.* (Our clue, for example, to the Second Coming must be the first one.) In other words, we apply to the life beyond death the great argument of St Paul: 'He who did not spare his own Son but gave him up for us all, will he not also give us all things with him . . . For I am persuaded that neither death nor life . . . will be able to separate us from the love of God in Christ Jesus our Lord' (Rom. 8.32, 38f.). Our Christian belief in a blessed life hereafter is thus an inference from the doctrine of our redemption. The God who cared, and cares, for us, will care for us for ever – care for us till past all darkness, danger and death, we shall see him 'face to face'.

Second, *for St John, his visions of heaven were the fruit not of his own untutored imagination but of the revealing Spirit of God.* 'I was in the Spirit on the Lord's Day', he tells us at the beginning of his book, and at the end, 'In the Spirit he carried me away to a great high mountain.' Now, since it is the Holy Spirit's work to

146

'take of the things of Christ and show them' to his followers and to 'declare what is to come' (John 16.13f.), it follows that John's pictures of 'Jerusalem the Golden' were inspired by the Spirit of God. To be sure, they take the form of highly-coloured visions – what many would call 'myths'. 'Myths' they may be, but, as a poet has said:

> Myth is the language that contains the clue
> To that which is at once both real and true.

Provided we remember that John's visions are not charts of heaven but inspired instructions to faith, they may still today speak to us of the nature of that 'hope which is laid up for us in heaven'.

What have they to tell us?

First, at the end of the Christian road is a city – the city of God. In other words, the consummation of the Christian hope is supremely *social*. It is not a 'flight of the alone to the Alone' but life in the redeemed community of heaven (see Rev. 7.9–17). More, heaven means belonging for ever to the great family of God: 'I will be his God, and he shall be my son' (Rev. 21.7)

Next, whatever else heaven means, it means an end to all the sorrows and evils of earth. 'God,' says the heavenly voice, 'will wipe away every tear from their eyes, and death shall be no more, neither shall there be mourning nor crying nor any pain any more, for the former things have passed away' (Rev. 21.4).

Finally, heaven must mean the Beatific Vision. When John says, 'They shall see his face' (Rev. 22.4), he but echoes his Lord's beatitude, 'Blessed are the pure in heart, for they shall see God' (Matt. 5.8).

To behold the God before whom angels veil their faces, the God who created us and, in Christ, redeemed us, who so loved his lost and wandering children that he came right down among us to show us what he is like and then by the cross of his dear Son saved us from our sins and made us heirs of life eternal, and, beholding him, to behold all things in him and in the light of his redemption, this truly,

were a well spent journey
Though seven deaths lay between.

And, if they serve to purify our spirits for this inconceivable reward of God's grace, the sufferings and sorrows of this life will not seem altogether meaningless or vain. To see God and his Son – the Lamb that once was slain – face to face amid the fellowship of the church triumphant, this surely is the end of all ends, the final solution to life's riddle, and the consummation of all love and desire.